KOBE BRYANT'S SNEAKER HISTORY

(1996-2020)

PAT BENSON

Copyright © 2020 by Pat Benson
All rights reserved. This book or any portion thereof
may not be reproduced or used in any manner whatsoever
without the express written permission of the publisher
except for the use of brief quotations in a book review.

Printed in the United States of America

First Printing, 2020

Paperback ISBN: 978-1-7359409-0-8
Ebook ISBN: 978-1-7359409-1-5

Baggy Shorts Press
Editor: Meredith Spears
Formatting: Enchanted Ink Publsihing

To my parents
Jan and Pat Sr.

And the love of my life
Lynn.

CONTENTS

1   Chapter 1: Fresh Prince

13   Chapter 2: California Love

21   Chapter 3: Free Agency

28   Chapter 4: The Swoosh

34   Chapter 5: Black Mamba

48   Chapter 6: Ringsssss

61   Chapter 7: Lows

76   Chapter 8: Highs

86   Chapter 9: Arrivederci

96   Chapter 10: Rebirth

110   Chapter 11: #GirlDad

FOREWORD

I hardly remember any shopping experiences. For me, it's a necessary evil. Get in and get out, and try not to let a well-meaning sales assistant upsell you on something you don't need. But there is one mall visit I will never forget. On Tuesday, June 7, 2016, I waited outside the doors of my local mall, itching to get inside. The night before, my paycheck hit my checking account via direct deposit, and I was ready to do some damage.

Finally, the doors opened, and I speed-walked past the stay-at-home moms and senior citizens in the direction of the retail store Footaction. The escalator wasn't moving fast enough, so I was that guy skipping down the steps. Somehow, a sneakerhead I knew from the college I worked at was already outside the store. I was confused on how he'd beat me there. Do sneakerheads respawn inside the mall each morning? He must have recognized the look in my eyes, because he said, "Oh, Pat is about to buy some shoes! Let me know if you need some help picking them out!"

Nah, I'm good, man. There was zero doubt about what I was about to purchase. The Nike Kobe 11 EM in the "Draft Day" colorway. Far from the most-hyped Kobe sneaker of all time, or even that model. I didn't care about any of that. For the past few weeks, I had watched dozens of unboxing videos, scoured official promo photos, and read countless posts on the message board *NikeTalk*.

So many things about that colorway intrigued me. Of course, the storytelling—in one of the worst trades of all time, the Charlotte Hornets drafted Kobe Bryant only to trade him to the Los Angeles Lakers for Vlade Divac. Thus, the sneaker came in Hornets colors—white, teal, and purple. Or, as Nike called it, "White/Blue-Lagoon/Court Purple." But the details were what really blew my mind: the "Sheath" Kobe logo on the tongue, the speckled laces, the red stitches on the left heel (a nod to Bryant's Achilles surgery), and the draft date on the right heel.

At 11:01 a.m., I ran into Footaction and made a beeline toward the back corner of the store. Out of breath, I pointed at the wall and asked the team member, "Do y'all have that shoe in a size thirteen?"

Startled by dramatic appearance, he said, "Uh, let me check in the back."

After what felt like forever, he reappeared holding a black-and-white striped box under his arm. I let out a sigh of relief and quickly tried them on to confirm they fit (shout out to all the YouTubers who already made that clear).

It was a wrap. I put the sneakers back in the box and headed to the cash register. No coupons, no discounts, nothing. I was a newb and was happy to drop $160 plus taxes. Per their store policy, the team member tried to sell me some insoles to replace the teal Lunarlon insoles with ones that had little Kobe Logos all over them (that was a hard no from me). Then he asked if I was going to hoop in the new sneakers. Again, that was a hard no from me.

Timeout. I know that's blasphemous, but you have to understand how badly I wanted to keep the white outsoles clean. I went as far as to buy clear protectors that stuck to the bottom of the outsole to keep them clean from a company called SOLE PROTECTOR.

Once I got back to my apartment, I studied the sneakers like they were ancient hieroglyphics. The dots on the side known as "Kobe Code"; the date on the back of the right heel that read "6.11.96."

Wait a second. That wasn't the date of the 1996 NBA Draft. The back of the right heel was supposed to read "6.26.96."

I frantically Googled it only to learn the history of the "Draft Day" colorway. A manufacturing error resulted in the wrong date on many of the Kobe 4s. Apparently, Nike had some fun with it on the Kobe 11, and I got a pair of the "rare errors." I took multiple pictures of the sneakers from different angles before immediately posting them to Instagram.

I laced them up and went into work. I'm sure my bosses weren't thrilled, but that was their problem, not mine. All the student-workers in the call center I managed got hyped *for me*. "Ay, Pat finally did it!" and "Those are clean!" I know, I know. I felt like a different man when I had Kobes on my feet. Hell, I *was* a different man with Kobes on my feet. I felt braver, tougher, surlier—more like the Black Mamba.

It might sound crazy to some people, but Kobe Bryant had more of an impact on me than any other man outside my family, and I'd never even met the guy. Like so many other people reading this book, he sacrificed everything to give us twenty years in the NBA. In his words, we asked for his hustle, and he gave us his heart. His play excited us, his words inspired us, and his mentality drove us.

When Bryant came into the league, it was a breath of fresh air. It wasn't always easy growing up in southeast Tennessee in the 1990s as Catholic, Democrat, West Coast basketball fan. Besides my dad, I'd never even known another Lakers fan until I met my friend Volonte on the first day of sixth grade. That mutual interest sparked a friendship that lasted nearly two decades.

I kept up with Bryant's every move, but I was never a sneakerhead. I wore my old team shoes from high school when I wanted to hoop and sandals the rest of the time. Plus, $160+ is a lot of money. But I had a grownup job now and a new addiction to feed—sneakers. I went crazy on the Kobe 11, chasing that flyknit dragon. "Carpe Diem," "Bruce Lee," and the "Eulogy" colorways in quick order. *Boom. Boom. Boom.* Luckily for my bank account, I eventually calmed down. No more than one colorway per model.

Following Bryant's retirement, it was inspiring to see him dominate industries that had little to do with basketball. Even better, it was heartwarming to see him finally get some time with his family.

Like the rest of the world, the events of January 26, 2020 shook me to my core. That day seems like a blur. As the tributes flooded social media, I remember Barack Obama's tweet. It read, "Kobe was a legend on the court and just getting started in what would have been just as meaningful a second act. To lose Gianna is even more heartbreaking to us as parents. Michelle and I send love and prayers to Vanessa and the entire Bryant family on an unthinkable day."

Man, I broke down and started crying tears that never seemed to stop. The following day, Monday, I sat at my desk and cried my eyes out for eight straight hours. Our hero, our champion, our philosopher, was gone in a blink of an eye. To drive the knife further into our hearts, his daughter Gianna and seven other passengers were gone too. So many unfulfilled dreams and possibilities.

2020 got even worse from there. My longtime friend and fellow Kobe-fanatic, Volonte, died in a car wreck the night before Kobe and Gianna's public memorial. I found out at work the following day, a Monday again. And for the second time in as many months, I cried my eyes out at work. I bounced back and forth between grief for my hero and my friend. As the months rolled by and the pandemic worsened, I was laid off from my two side hustles and eventually my day job. My parents and fiancée suggested I write a book about something I'm passionate about that would also entertain readers.

So, I'm typing this on an old MacBook Pro in my apartment amid a nationwide quarantine during a global pandemic. I'm nowhere near the biggest Kobe sneakerhead. A lot of you reading this have a much stronger collection than me. And every one of you reading this has your own story about what got you into Kobes. But my goal for this book is to document the sneaker history of one of the most influential basketball players in the history of the game.

I hope anybody who reads this book is not only entertained but finds some inspiration through the stories of Kobe Bryant's undeniable will. Most importantly, I hope you reach success at success at success.

Pat Benson

CHAPTER 1

Fresh Prince

On June 15, 1996, Kobe Bryant stood before a podium in the gym at Lower Merion High School. The skinny, 6'6" kid wore a brown suit, white shirt, patterned tie, and sunglasses sitting atop his freshly shaved head. As light bulbs flashed and fans cheered, Bryant took a moment to pretend to struggle with the decision that had been made months before the announcement.

"I have decided to skip college and take my talent to the NBA," said the seventeen-year-old phenom.

The crowd erupted in excitement before he could complete the sentence. It was a scene fit for a superstar. Few people could successfully pull off such an event, and even fewer could dream of leap-frogging college to go straight to a physically demanding league.

Bryant's elite skill set and self-confidence were rooted in his historic work ethic. His unique upbringing molded him into a prodigy built for the limelight. Bryant's father, Joe "Jelly Bean" Bryant, had played in the NBA before finishing his career in Italy. Growing up in a foreign country had a tremendous influence on Bryant's personality. His time in Italy impacted everything from the language he spoke to his cultural tastes.

There is no doubt Bryant wanted to compete against the best players in the world. But skipping college could have done irreparable damage to his professional career had he not been physically prepared for the grueling schedule or mentally tough enough for the harsh media criticism. Bryant's unrelenting belief in himself was the main reason for bypassing college. However, the importance of securing a lucrative sneaker contract served as a significant factor in his decision.

Legendary sports marketing executive Sonny Vaccaro was instrumental in facilitating Bryant's first sneaker contract. Vaccaro had previously worked for Nike, where he signed a young Michael Jordan to the company. After an acrimonious breakup with Nike, Vaccaro began working for Adidas, where he was in charge of finding the nation's top young talent.

In July of 1994, Vaccaro was running Adidas's elite, invitation-only ABCD camp. In the book *Showboat: The Life of Kobe Bryant*, biographer Roland Lazenby described a scene where Joe Bryant showed up in person to campaign for his son's acceptance into the exclusive basketball camp.[1]

Despite an excellent sophomore season, Bryant was still unknown on the national scene and had not garnered an invitation to either the Nike or Adidas camps. Thanks to Vaccaro's familiarity with Joe Bryant (a previous MVP of his 1972 Dapper Dan high school all-star tournament), the executive allowed the unproven prospect into his camp. It would not take long for Bryant to impress Vaccaro. So much so that Vaccaro began to dream big of Bryant's potential. The 1994 Adidas camp started a relationship between Vaccaro and the Bryant family for years to come.

Throughout Bryant's junior and senior season, the rail-thin prospect flourished into an undeniable talent. Every game for Lower Merion, his AAU team, and camp appearance served as an opportunity for Bryant to impose his will with the ball. Letters, phone calls, and recruiting visits from the nation's top college programs inundated the prospect. All the while, Vaccaro made his plans for making Bryant the future face of Adidas in the NBA. By the fall of 1995, Vaccaro teamed up with Gary Charles to secure a secret deal with Bryant.[2] Charles, a former AAU coach, was friends with Joe Bryant and attended Lower Merion games. It took months, but eventually, the two parties agreed Bryant would go pro and sign a contract with Adidas.

What resulted was an unprecedented deal for a high school kid who was far from a sure thing: a multi-year contract for $10 million with more than $1 million guaranteed for Kobe, while Joe would receive $150,000 to become an Adidas "employee."[3] The terms of the agreement were quietly finalized in March of 1996 and inked weeks later. It was an important cash windfall for the Bryant family. From that point forward, Bryant's goal was finding the right NBA team to fit both his hoop dreams and budding brand.

Vaccaro assisted in building Kobe's team, which included Rick Bradley with the William Morris Agency and sports agent Arn Tellem. Bradley was in charge of entertainment. At the same time, Tellem was focused on the NBA contract.[4] After weeks of gamesmanship and backchanneling, the Charlotte Hornets drafted Kobe Bryant with the thirteenth overall pick before trading him to the Los Angeles Lakers for Vlade Divac. The kid with a smile that could light up an arena was heading to Tinseltown. It was a match made in heaven.

Adidas EQT

The league Bryant entered at the beginning of the 1996-1997 season was unrecognizable compared to the league he retired from after the 2015-2016 season. Michael Jordan ruled the NBA and most of the global sports landscape. His iconic sneaker line, dubbed "Air Jordan," was revolutionary in its technology and popularity. However, the Lakers had no shortage of star power. Recently acquired All-Star center Shaquille O'Neal was immensely popular. In addition to ripping down backboards, O'Neal was a marketing wunderkind. By his mid-twenties, he had recorded rap albums, appeared in movies, and had a signature sneaker line with Reebok.

Alongside O'Neal, point guard Nick Van Exel was also a signature athlete with Reebok. Meanwhile, one of the team's flashiest players, shooting guard Eddie Jones, wore Jordan-brand sneakers. He was part of a select few of Jordan's contemporaries to be branded "Team Jordan" and wear models such as the Jordan Jumpman Quick 6 or the Jordan Jumpman Swift 6.

All three of those players were All-Stars with strong marketing powers thanks to their play style and residing in the entertainment capital of the world. A lesser man might have gladly taken a backseat to the more established veterans in front of him, but Bryant, at eighteen years old, was insistent on becoming the focal point of the team.

Throughout the season, he would often annoy his teammates with his self-assured attitude that bordered on cockiness. Bryant would come off the bench for 65 of the 71 games he played in during his rookie season. He wore several new Adidas sneakers from the EQT line that used "Feet You Wear" technology created by Frampton Ellis. Feet You Wear focused on the foot's sole to create a more balanced ride and protect from ankle injuries.[5] Its quintessentially 90s logo highlighted the pressure points of the foot and looked like a cartoon face. Marketing gimmicks aside, the Feet You Wear technology is still being used to this day.

Few people are as well-versed in Adidas history as Matt Welty, associate editor of *Complex Sneakers*, co-host of internet show *Full Size Run*, and co-host of *The Complex Sneakers Podcast*. About the Feet You Wear technology, Welty says, "Adidas has always been a tech-driven company, since the days of putting a computer in the Micropacer in 1984 or using adjustable cushioning in shoes such as the LA Trainer. Marketing the tech, for the German company, has been the problem. Feet You Wear was easy to understand and made sense to consumers, to some degree, and that's shown in the tech's lasting legacy."[6]

Bryant wasn't the only Adidas signature athlete to wear Feet You Wear footwear. NFL wide receiver Keyshawn Johnson and tennis player Steffi Graf also wore the new Adidas technology. Welty gives some important context: "There's a touch of nostalgia for the Key Trainer, Keyshawn Johnson's signature shoe. However, its retro in 2014 didn't gain much traction outside of a core group of sneaker fanatics who still obsessed over Eastbay catalogs. The Kobe sneakers are the definable pop culture moment for the shoes, including wearing the EQT Elevation in the 1997 NBA Dunk Contest."[7]

Bryant wore three Adidas models throughout his rookie season: Top Ten 2000, Top Ten 2010, and EQT Elevation.[8] The Top Ten 2000 is seen in the iconic picture of Bryant working out in Celtics gear before the 1996 NBA Draft. Additionally, one of Bryant's earliest commercials showed him wearing the Top Ten 2000.[9] In the ad, Bryant is practicing both in the sneaker and barefoot while he touts speed being the best part of his game. The model used a synthetic leather upper material with elastic straps to kept the foot locked into place and a herringbone outsole for gripping onto the hardwood.[10]

The Top Ten 2010 made modest improvements upon its predecessor, the Top Ten 2000—similar materials and design, albeit sleeker with more pronounced branding. The three-stripe logo with the Feet You Wear face were much more visible throughout the sneaker.

Finally, the sneaker made popular in the 1997 Slam Dunk contest, the EQT Elevation. The EQT Elevation again featured a synthetic leather upper, molded EVA midsole, but this time with a holographic logo on the ankle and design, which lent itself to more customizations.[11]

Bryant swaggered onto the court, still wearing his shooting shirt and a fresh pair of EQT Elevation PEs (player exclusive) designed in a Lakers colorway. Purple, black, white, and a gold holographic logo that had Bryant's number 8 shining back at the cameras. After throwing down a blizzard of eye-popping dunks and hamming it up for the fans, Bryant was crowned the 1997 NBA Slam Dunk Contest Champion. His star power was now undeniable.

That same year Bryant appeared in an Adidas commercial for the EQT Elevation. In the ad, Bryant is sitting outside on an unusually rainy day in Southern California. He begins talking trash to his friends before the sun comes out and torches them in a streetball game on the courts at Venice Beach.[12] The streetball scene makes sense given the time. Fellow rookie Allen Iverson of the Philadelphia 76ers was ushering in a new era of culture and style that appealed to the young basketball fans on the streets some would call the "Hip-Hop Generation." In fact, Iverson already had his own signature sneaker with Reebok.

The Lakers' 1997 season concluded with an unceremonious playoff exit at the hands of the Utah Jazz, where Bryant heaved up four air balls in five minutes. Bryant's detractors saw it as a moment of weakness, whereas many (including teammate Shaquille O'Neal) saw it as courage and strength. O'Neal wrapped his giant arm around the skinny teenager and consoled him as the two walked off the court of the Delta Center.

KB8

The summer of 1997 was crucial for the development of the rising sophomore. After the "air ball game" in Utah, Bryant was hyper-focused on preparing his body for the grind of an 82-game regular season plus a playoff run. According to filmmaker Spike Lee, that's why Bryant passed on the role of Jesus Shuttlesworth in the movie *He Got Game*.[13] Ray Allen, who was also going into his second year in the league, ended up getting the part in the Spike Lee Joint. Despite passing on the role, there would be plenty of marketing opportunities for Bryant in the future—including working with Spike Lee later in his career. In addition to putting on some muscle, Bryant ditched the shaved head for a cooler mini-afro and goatee, which made him look more like a leading role in a 1970s action movie rather than a young Michael Jordan.

After showing moments of brilliance during his rookie season, Adidas was ready to move forward with the development of Bryant's first signature shoe: the Adidas KB8. Again, this model was part of the Feet You Wear line and certainly had more style than what Bryant had previously worn on the court. The KB8 used high-quality leather that helped the distinctive contour curves near the bottom of the sneaker pop. The colorways were kept simple, mostly black and white. There was only a touch of purple on the Adidas branding, the pull-tabs, and on the outsole, which was hardly visible.

Adidas ditched the elastic straps with this sneaker and relied on the foam curves and inner bootie to help keep the foot locked into place.[14] What didn't change with this shoe was the EVA midsole and the traditional herringbone outsole. Another distinct feature on the outsole was the TORSION technology that Adidas used in other non-basketball shoes since 1988.[15] TORSION used a TPU arch to connect the heel to the forefront for more stability and theoretically reduce foot fatigue. Supporting the arch of the foot with a piece of plastic or carbon fiber has become a mainstay in basketball footwear since that time.

Like most basketball sneakers of that era, the KB8 offered eyelets to lace all the way up your ankle. Despite its clunky appearance, the sneaker only weighed twelve ounces, which was a departure from the boxy footwear of that era. The KB8 did an impressive job of marrying technology and visual appeal.

A commercial for the KB8 depicts Bryant practicing in a cavernous warehouse on an incredibly high rim. Ominous voices heckle and question the young superstar. Soon monsters, ghosts, and even a giant bug taunt an unfazed Bryant cutting through the noise. Finally, as the madness crescendos, Bryant swishes the shot and silences the villains. He looks directly into the camera and says, "Just believe in yourself," then walks away as the Adidas logo appears on the screen.[16] Jeers and solitude were not part of Hollywood fiction, as the teenager was still struggling to fit in with his older teammates.

Rudy Garciduenas was the Lakers Equipment Manager when Bryant entered the league and worked closely with him until parting ways with the team in 2011. When I asked about Bryant's early years with Adidas, Garciduenas recalled, "I remember how excited he was when he started his own shoe branding. He had the biggest smile when he would talk to you about his footwear." Garciduenas continued, "The Top Tens were still the traditional Adidas styling, but he was able to create something more unique with the EQT and KB8s. He really loved that."[17]

Building off an All-Rookie NBA Second Team selection, Bryant was ready to take his game to the next level. The problem was that he was still stuck behind Eddie Jones and only started in one of the 79 games he played in during the 1997-1998 season. Bryant may not have been a starter on a playoff-contending team yet, but he had earned more playing time. During his sophomore season, his averages jumped from 15.5 to 26 minutes per game and 7.6 to 15.4 points per game compared to his rookie campaign.

His game's improvement was on full display in a duel with Michael Jordan and the Bulls in Chicago on December 17, 1997. Coming off the bench, Bryant put up 33 points to Jordan's 36 points. Thanks to his bravado and acrobatic dunks, Bryant's popularity soared. In just his second season, Bryant became the youngest player to be voted an NBA All Star. What's more, he got over 90,000 more votes than teammate Eddie Jones.

The 1998 NBA All-Star Game took place in New York City. Teammates Eddie Jones, Nick Van Exel, and Shaquille O'Neal were also voted in by fans to play for the Western Conference team. Four All-Stars from the same team had not happened since 1983. Before the weekend festivities began, Adidas made a concerted effort to use this opportunity to market Bryant. Full-page advertisements in newspapers and magazine covers further elevated the youngest NBA All-Star Game starter in league history.

The same year, Adidas released a rare promotional kit that celebrated the stupendous sophomore. For fans lucky enough to get their hands on the box, it contained promotional photos, a T-shirt, and a "Virtual Kobe" CD-ROM. After popping the CD-ROM into your computer, a series of commercials played that showed Bryant practicing, playing with children, and cutting up with his sister.[18]

Friend of the Bryant family and *SLAM* Magazine contributor Anthony Gilbert knew Kobe and his sister Shariya since the early 90s. No reporter covered Bryant for as long as Gilbert. The Philadelphia-native saw Bryant through all stages of his life. Plus, he was in attendance for many of the most important moments of Bryant's career.

Gilbert fondly recalled Bryant's early years with Adidas. "Like his first couple of shoes, his ad campaigns and creative marketing were very relatable and genuine. He still had his Philly accent, and he was so young, which really helped his overall brand. There wasn't a kid who didn't look up to him or try to emulate his game and style of play. The commercials with his oldest sister are very authentic, and it reminds me so much of our time growing up together."[19]

Unfortunately, the bubble would burst on Bryant's dream season. The Lakers went 61-21 during the regular season, and rolled through the Trail Blazers and SuperSonics in the playoffs, only to be swept by the Jazz in a tidy four-game series. Bryant finished second in voting for the 1998 Sixth Man of the Year Award. His talent was unquestionable, but what would soon be in doubt was the future of the young core.

KB8 II

The 1998-1999 NBA season was one of the most consequential periods in Bryant's career. One month after being swept by the Jazz, the Lakers traded Nick Van Exel to the Nuggets. A labor dispute resulted in a lockout and shortened the season to just 50 games. Due to the shortened season, the 1999 All-Star Game in Philadelphia never took place. After 20 games Eddie Jones got traded to the Hornets. Not to mention, the Lakers signed and eventually released Dennis Rodman after 23 games. Oh, and the team cycled through three head coaches: Del Harris, Bill Bertka, and Kurt Rambis.

Despite the turbulence, Bryant thrived in his third season. He started all 50 games, averaged nearly 38 minutes per game, and scored almost 20 points per game. His performance earned him a six-year contract extension with the Lakers and made All-NBA Third Team. Fans were looking for an heir to the recently retired Michael Jordan, and it was crystal clear Bryant was the new face of the league. Not Eddie Jones, not Penny Hardaway, not Grant Hill, but the shot-happy, self-assured youngster who grew up in Italy. Meanwhile, Adidas released the second installment of his signature shoe, the KB8 II. Adidas continued down the same path of incorporating Feet You Wear technology and slimming down the shoe for a more natural fit.

The outsole focused on pressure points and took on an even more rounded shape for stability. However, the KB8 II used a multi-directional pattern segmented and highlighted by different colors. Additionally, the Torsional system remained intact. For the cushion, Adidas went with an EVA midsole and heavily padded ankle collar on the sneaker's interior. The design team kept the wavy contours along the midsole and added a more breathable upper consisting of synthetics and mesh with reflective 3M piping covering the sneaker.[20] The Adidas Logo remained prominently featured on the ankle collar and tongue. Colorways were simple, alternating between black and white with purple accents around the sneaker.

The commercial filmed for the KB8 II went back to a streetball appeal. This time the Lakers jersey was replaced with a sleeveless gray shirt and black shorts. Spectators watched through a chain-link fence as Bryant sliced through defenders. After leaping off the ground, Bryant hung in the air for ten seconds while he debated with himself on which move to pull off before deciding on a flashy pass to an open teammate. The commercial ended with Bryant backpedaling with a grin on his face as the Adidas logo appeared on screen.[21]

The Lakers chaotic season ended by getting swept in the Western Conference Semi-Finals by the Spurs. It would be the last Lakers game in the Great Western Forum, and the end of coming up short in the playoffs. The 1998-1999 season was a disaster for the team, but it was an inflection point in Bryant's career. Through all of the noise he transformed himself from an ambitious prodigy to a certified assassin on the court.

KB8 III

If the 1998-1999 season was a nightmare for the Lakers, then the 1999-2000 season would be a daydream. The turnaround began with the hiring of legendary coach Phil Jackson. The "Zen Master" had overseen the Bulls dynasty with Michael Jordan, which netted him six rings.

Lakers owner Jerry Buss and General Manager Jerry West needed a veteran coach who was able to manage young stars with big egos. Jackson had done just that in Chicago with Michael Jordan, Scottie Pippen, and Dennis Rodman.

In addition to practicing meditation and yoga, Jackson implemented the triangle offense that revolved around court spacing and players reading the defense before reacting. The strategy emphasized teamwork over isolation. It took the ball out of Michael Jordan's hands in Chicago, and it quickly took the ball out of Bryant's hands in Los Angeles. As is the case between dominant personalities, Jackson and his dynamic duo would not always see eye to eye, but he proved to be the final ingredient needed for a championship run.

Bringing Phil Jackson to Los Angeles was vital for the development of Kobe Bryant. But Jackson was a distant second to the most important person Bryant would meet that year—seventeen-year-old Vanessa Laine. Bryant's dabbling in hip-hop is well-documented and often ridiculed. However, on a fateful day in November of 1999, he met his future wife on a music video set. The two kids fell head over heels in love with each other and quickly became soulmates. Vanessa was Kobe's best friend and confidante. For a young superstar who always had trouble fitting in, he had finally found his prize. The positive impact she had on him was unquantifiable. Their bond would prove to be unbreakable.

Bryant had finally found the stability he needed both on the court and at home. But now he was cycling through sneakers throughout this all-important season. Bryant debuted the KB8 III at the end of the previous season and started the new season with them on foot.

The latest model kept the curvy contours around the midsole and went with a much simpler and sleeker look up top—a leather upper with three stripes that popped, and a patch of suede that cupped the back of the sneaker (with an Adidas logo). Bryant wore colorways including black, white, and platinum, with hints of Lakers colors on the accents.

The technology was similar to its predecessors, and that was the problem. A licensing dispute between Adidas and the creator of Feet You Wear caused a halt in the production of products that used the proprietary technology.[22] But that wasn't before some memorable advertisements captured Bryant in the sneaker.

You have likely seen the KB8 III many times without ever noticing them. While Bryant was recovering from a broken hand in the fall of 1999, he went out onto the court to get shots up with his left hand. What often distracts from that session's photos was what he was wearing—his gold practice uniform with his flannel pajama bottoms underneath his shorts. Most people look at the cast on his right hand or the baggy pajamas. But if you look closely, a white pair of KB8 III sneakers are included in the photos.

In addition to the legendary pajama practice session, the KB8 III gave us one of the funniest sneaker commercials since Nike's Lil' Penny series. In the ad, a kid is practicing on UCLA's basketball court before calling out for Kobe to give him a game of one-on-one.

Bryant explains to the camera how he doesn't believe in cutting people slack, while the kid confidently explains his game's strong points (speed, shot, stamina, integrity). All the while, clips roll of Bryant relentlessly blocking the kid's shot into the stands. "I'm going to shake him up bad," proclaims the kid as Kobe flies over him to two-hand dunk as the commercial concludes.[23] It was good acting and even better comedy.

Bryant also wore the KB8 III in a Spalding commercial that aired in 1999. In the advertisement, Bryant, clad in the Lakers home uniform, performs fancy dribbling moves while talking candidly to the camera.

Bryant says, "People always ask me, 'Kobe, why did you go pro so quickly? Was it destiny? Was it fame and fortune? Why would a kid from Philly risk it all in LA?' Do you really want to know?"

Each question punctuated with clips of Bryant performing spectacular moves in games, before cutting back to him dribbling the ball on set.

"I just wanted to play with this," he says as he palms the ball towards the camera to give viewers a closer look. "Spalding is the official ball of the NBA. What are you playing?"[24]

One of the final advertisements we saw of Bryant wearing the KB8 III was on the cover of the Nintendo 64 video game titled "NBA Courtside 2 featuring Kobe Bryant." The video game cover showed Bryant in the middle of a backward dunk with the ball held below his waist. Look to the left of his bent knees, and you'll see a pair of KB8 IIIs in a white-and-black colorway.[25] It was the second consecutive year he'd graced the cover of the video game series, but the product placement for Adidas in the game that released on November 8, 1999 was perfect.

Now that the KB8 line was over, Bryant needed a sneaker to hold him over until Adidas revealed the next big thing for the face of their basketball line. Being a man with an appreciation for classics, Bryant wore the Adidas Forum 2000.[26] It was an updated take on the classic hoop shoe from 1984. The straightforward sneaker had no frills and most often used a simple black-and-white colorway. Bryant still put up some amazing performances in the placeholder. Ironically enough, Bryant never wore the Forum 2000 in the Great Western Forum. During the summer of 1999, the Lakers had moved from Inglewood to Downtown Los Angeles and opened the state-of-the-art Staples Center. The iconic arena housed the Lakers and Clippers, as well as the NHL's Los Angeles Kings.

With the new home came new uniforms. The Lakers moved away from their showtime-era uniforms with the rounded collar and drop-shadow numbers. Now the uniforms featured an updated Lakers script across the chest, white numbers on the gold jerseys, and a wishbone collar along with other tweaks to the classic uniforms.[27] It was a modern uniform fit for the new century and new chapters of Lakers history. Times were changing—not only for the Lakers but the league. Jordan had retired, Jackson was in Los Angeles, and Adidas was ready to shock the world with a new sneaker.

CHAPTER 2

California Love

The Kobe

Everything came together perfectly for the Lakers in the 1999-2000 season. O'Neal led the team to a 67-15 regular season record and earned the NBA Most Valuable Player Award and was named All-NBA First Team and NBA All-Defensive Second Team. The big man was without a doubt in the best shape of his career. He started in all 79 games he played and averaged 40 minutes per game. His play style was brutal—29.7 points, 13.6 rebounds, and 3.03 blocks per game.

Bryant started in 62 of 66 games, averaging 22.5 points, 6.3 rebounds, 4.9 assists, and 1.6 steals per game. Those numbers put him on the All-NBA Second Team and NBA All-Defensive First Team. Before the two All-Stars were crowned Western Conference champions, they had to face one final obstacle—the Portland Trail Blazers. The series required seven games and a heroic fourth-quarter comeback in Staples Center. The Lakers clawed their way back from a 15-point deficit and clinched the game after an alley-oop from Bryant to O'Neal. No fan in the Staples Center could contain themselves.

Even Bob Costas of NBC lit up with excitement: *Bryant to SHAQ!* before being drowned out by fans.

The Indiana Pacers won the Eastern Conference championship thanks to the veteran leadership of Reggie Miller and the steady hand of Coach Larry Bird. But that Lakers team was ready to make history. The Lakers won the 2000 NBA Finals in a 4-2 series, and the championship drought was over for the franchise. O'Neal's dominant performance secured the NBA Finals Most Valuable Player Award. But Bryant had arrived. He was an NBA champion. And Adidas could not have picked a better time to have their star athlete debut his radical new sneaker—The Kobe.

Inspired by the Audi TT Roadster, Peter Moore went for something that had never been done before. It was a basketball sneaker that looked more like a vehicle than performance footwear. The curvy contours of the KB8 line were gone. In their place, boxy side panels donned three barely visible stripes. A shell toe and foam ankle collars completed the synthetic upper. The Kobe kept the herringbone traction pattern and Torsion system for support and stability.[28] Colorways were monochromatic—all white, all black, or all silver, with the occasional all gold. It was a futuristic sneaker that made sense in the year 2000. However, as time passed, sneakerheads would have varied opinions on the polarizing model.

Adidas leaned into the vehicle theme with one specific commercial for the sneaker. A daring man on a motorcycle flies down a mountainside, weaving through Los Angeles traffic, before arriving at the Staples Center. The camera centers on the shiny, all-black sneaker that matches the leather suit of the daredevil. The motorist takes off his helmet, revealing Bryant. With a sly grin on his face, Bryant walks toward the camera as he enters the arena. The word "KOBE" appears onscreen before fading to the Adidas logo with "Adidas" sitting on top of "FOREVER SPORT."

Another ad from the same campaign includes Bryant sitting in an Italian villa clad in an Adidas jumpsuit with The Kobe on his feet. As church bells ring and birds chirp, Bryant sits back and pontificates on matters such as creativity, emotions, and self-confidence. He scratches his head and rubs his chin, looking off in the distance. He narrates the commercial, saying:

> *I think creativity comes from within. I think everybody is born with creativity, but I believe it's the trust in yourself and the trust in your emotions to talk to yourself, so to speak—to become your own psychologist. To let your emotions out on a piece of paper. To not be afraid of anything. To not be afraid of what people think. To not be afraid of what people may say. To just be yourself—and I think that is something that is rare nowadays.*

The third and final commercial for The Kobe shows Bryant sitting in a practice gym while awaiting an important event. Boredom kicks in and he starts shooting a paper ball into a trash can as he talks to himself. Eventually, the suit coat comes off and a real basketball gets pulled out. "Fourth quarter, and the Lakers are down by five," Bryant whispers to himself as he gives up on the event in order to simulate a game-scenario.[29]

The Kobe hit stores several months after their debut. Full-page ads showed Bryant in a baggy Adidas jumpsuit, reclining into a lounge chair with his eyes closed. Above him, a giant, The Kobe sneaker in a white colorway stared down at him. The print below read, "The KOBE found at select stores 12.15.2000."[30] By this time, both parties had lived up to their expectations of marketing. Adidas sent Bryant all around the world to build an international fanbase, while Bryant dutifully attended every event asked of him.

But there was trouble in paradise between Team Bryant and Adidas. In the book *Showboat: The Life of Kobe Bryant*, biographer Roland Lazenby details several issues that hurt Bryant's relationship with Adidas. There were manufacturing problems and delays with The Kobe. The design resulted in a rigid and uncomfortable sneaker. To further complicate matters, Bryant's family was cooling off on Adidas. Vanessa, who married Kobe in April of 2001, wasn't a fan of the company. Plus, Joe Bryant was no longer part of the Adidas contract.[31]

One of the final times Bryant appeared in The Kobe was in a Spalding commercial that aired in 2002. Bryant, wearing the Lakers home uniform, charges into a space-age facility called the "Spalding Laboratory." He exclaims, "Professor, we have issues with this ball," as he slams a flat ball onto the floor only for it to not bounce back.

The scientist explains how the new Spalding Infusion Basketball contains a hidden micro-pump that allows players to increase the air pressure. The scientist passes the ball back to Bryant and warns, "Use caution, Number Eight. The Eastern Conference will stop at nothing to get this ball." Bryant immediately starts performing flashy dribbling moves, which gives viewers a clean look at the pair of The Kobes on his feet.[32]

Bryant continued to wear The Kobe throughout the 2000-2001 season. The Lakers easily coasted to a 56-26 regular season record and swept through the first three rounds of the playoffs. O'Neal and Bryant were once again All-Stars and named to multiple All-NBA teams. Bryant started in all 68 games he played in and bumped his scoring average up to 28.5 points per game. The only thing that changed on Bryant's feet were the colorways, and a special mesh edition of The Kobe released for the playoffs.

More important than the sneakers, Bryant got a chance to face off against Allen Iverson and the 76ers in the NBA Finals. Bryant had focused on Iverson since their rookie season. Iverson had won the 1997 NBA Rookie of the Year award. Reebok gave him a signature sneaker before Bryant got one from Adidas. Iverson had a stronger and more authentic connection to younger basketball fans. Not to mention, Iverson played in Bryant's hometown of Philadelphia.

It didn't take long for the fiery sides of both competitors to show. Iverson cooked the Lakers for 48 points in a Game 1 victory in Los Angeles. In Game 2, Bryant led the game with 31 points while Iverson was held in check for just 23 points. In the fourth quarter of Game 2, emotions boiled over as Bryant and Iverson got into a verbal altercation before teammates separated the two contemporaries. Despite Iverson's heroic performances, the Lakers were too much for the 76ers. The Lakers won the 2001 NBA Finals 4-1. O'Neal lifted the NBA Finals Most Valuable Player Trophy in Philadelphia on the floor of the First Union Center.

As celebrations took place in the locker room, a morose Bryant sat alone with the Larry O'Brien Trophy tucked under his arm. The gaudy championship jacket and matching hat couldn't cover up how he was feeling inside. A falling out with his parents left him melancholy during what should have been a homecoming celebration. The well-known photo of him sulking in the locker room is one of the enduring images from his career. What is lost on most people who view the picture is the pair of black The Kobes on his feet. Bryant's life was changing, and he would soon take more control of both the team and his business ventures.

The Kobe 2

The Kobe was groundbreaking and revolutionary in its appearance. Its successor, The Kobe 2, continued to build on the unorthodox design. The second model featured similar technology but an evolved upper. The three stripes on the lateral side were further minimized, the laces were completely hidden, and there was a silhouette of Kobe's head on the heel. Nearly two decades after The Kobe 2 was released, the model still looks futuristic.

Adidas continued to push both the sneaker and their athlete on TV. The commercial for The Kobe 2 was a minute of incredible, and in some cases, animated dunks.[33] What would be Bryant's final signature model with Adidas was available for retail on December 7, 2001 for $124.99.[34]

On opening night of the 2001-2002 season, an Afro-less Bryant debuted The Kobe 2 in a PE flag colorway that enveloped the entire sneaker. Following the terrorist attacks on September 11, 2001, the NBA and its players touted patriotism at every opportunity. Later that year, Bryant gave the patriotic PEs to a high school senior named LeBron James. In 2016, James told David McMenamin of ESPN, "I think I was playing in a tournament in Teaneck, New Jersey, and they were playing in the [2002] All-Star game in Philly. And I had an opportunity to go meet him, and he gave me a pair of his shoes, and I actually wore them in a game against Oak Hill, against Melo [Carmelo Anthony], actually."[35]

The 2002 NBA All-Star Game James spoke of meant a lot to Bryant. Just a week before, Lower Merion High School retired Bryant's number 33. However, the hometown kid received an icy reception from the Philadelphia fans during the All-Star Game. By the fourth quarter, it was clear Bryant would win the All-Star Game Most Valuable Player Award, and fans booed him every time he touched the ball. The 31-point performance did not please the crowd, who clearly wanted Allen Iverson to avenge the 2001 NBA Finals loss.

As Bryant fought back tears on the podium, you could see something happening. The seeds of embracing the villain role on the court had been planted. He ditched The Kobe 2s and wore The Kobe model for the final stretch of the season. Despite starting the season 14-1, the Lakers finished third in the Western Conference with a record of 58-24. Bryant started 80 games, averaged 25.2 points per game, and led the team in assists and steals. In addition to being named NBA All-Defensive Second Team, he was finally named All-NBA First Team alongside O'Neal.

The only thing standing in the way of a three-peat was a scary Sacramento Kings team. The Kings were a nightmare matchup for the Lakers. An intrastate rivalry had developed between the two teams over the previous few seasons. It would take a miracle buzzer-beater by Robert Horry in Game 4 and overtime victory in Game 7 for the Lakers to clinch the 2002 Western Conference Finals.

On the other side of the country, Jason Kidd and the New Jersey Nets coached by Byron Scott were the last team standing in the way of the Lakers and destiny. Thanks to another dominant performance by O'Neal, the Lakers swept the Nets to win the 2002 NBA Finals. After overcoming the Kings, the series against the Nets felt like a mere formality. There was hardly any celebration after the final buzzer in Game 4. O'Neal took his third-straight NBA Finals Most Valuable Player Award, Jackson tied Red Auerbach for most championships won as a coach, and the team prepared for yet another parade back in Los Angeles. It would be the final championship that Bryant and O'Neal won together. It would also be the last game we ever saw Bryant in an Adidas sneaker.

Summer of 2002

By this point in his career, Bryant was fully in control of making his own decisions. He had a new agent in Rob Pelinka and was ready to get out of his Adidas contract. In the book *Showboat: The Life of Kobe Bryant*, biographer Roland Lazenby depicts a terse meeting in Germany between Bryant and Adidas executives. Adidas laid out their vision for the future of Bryant's product line. Their plans included not only sneakers but a clothing line. But Bryant was upset with his signature sneaker line's direction and was ready to make another shrewd business move that would change the course of basketball sneaker history.[36]

Matt Welty of *Complex Sneakers* put the failed business relationship in a historical context: "Adidas's basketball history is interesting. They had the Pro Model and Superstar, then shoes like the Top 10, then they don't sign Jordan. The early 90s were tough for the brand, nearly going bankrupt. So signing Kobe seems big. And the brand still harps on it to this day. There were moments for them, but ultimately it all fell apart. To this day, Adidas still has a hard time figuring out basketball. Adidas and Kobe feel a lot more of 'what could have been' than the defining moments of Kobe's sneaker career."[37]

Basketball fans never got The Kobe 3 from Adidas. Thanks to the internet, pictures have surfaced of a wear-test sample of The Kobe 3. The model looks far less boxy and more of a marriage between the Adidas T-Mac 1 and Reebok Answer IV. Three stripes branding on the lateral side of the heel, a plastic toe cap, and overlay with a zipper to conceal the laces.

Without Bryant, the company ended up doubling down on the marketing of Tracy McGrady.

Welty notes, "It was the start of a different era for the brand. The company then focused more on its Originals line than performance shoes and those for athletes. Its basketball stuff post-Kobe is all forgettable. But even the Kobe-era wasn't all great for Adidas, as the Kobe Two was so bad it made him leave the brand."[38]

The Germany meeting was a failure for Adidas. Bryant cut ties with the same people who bet everything on him as a teenager. According to the *Wall Street Journal*, Bryant bought out the remainder of his Adidas contract for $8 million.[39] Before he eventually signed with Nike, Bryant used the 2002-2003 season as a sneaker free-agency period.

The first time the world saw Bryant in a new sneaker was that summer at an Entertainers Basketball Classic game at Rucker Park in Harlem, New York City. The historic outdoor basketball court served as the perfect launching pad for Bryant's sneaker free agency.

Basketball legends including Julius Erving, Kareem Abdul-Jabbar, and Wilt Chamberlain had all graced the outdoor court many years before Bryant. Plus, streetball was still riding a massive wave of popularity. Allen Iverson's flashy play style was a direct appeal to streetball.

The apparel company AND1 was mainstream at that time. So much so, ESPN aired the AND1 mixtape tour segments and the players became household names among young basketball fans.

In front of a standing-room-only crowd, Bryant stepped out onto the green court wearing an orange jersey that read "Entertainers" with the number 8. On his feet were a pair of Nike Air Force 1 Mids in a white-and-orange colorway. Every last detail was perfect. The sneakers known as "Uptowns" had long been a fashion staple in New York City. In November of that same year, rapper Nelly released a song titled "Air Force Ones" that fueled the popularity of an already classic sneaker.

Before the exhibition game was cut short due to rain, Bryant thrilled the crowd with an array of dunks and flashy dribbles. He tallied 15 points, seven assists, and seven rebounds. It was an electric start to what would be the beginning of a rebranding. Besides the memorable performance, some of Bryant's best nicknames came from the Rucker Park exhibition. MC Jeffery "Hannibal" Banks called Bryant "Lord of the Rings," "Kobe-wan Kenobi," "The Final Frontier," and "Junkyard Dog."[40] The hype man's wordplay stuck around for years to come.

Before the Lakers began their quest for a fourth consecutive title, legendary broadcaster Chick Hearn passed away at the age of 85. The play-by-play announcer for the Lakers had covered the team for 40 years and engrained himself in basketball lore. To pay tribute, the Lakers debuted white home uniforms on Christmas Day 2002. The white uniforms were meant only for Sundays and Christmas from that point forward. Not long before the season started, Bryant also learned he would soon be a father.

Everything was coming together for the twenty-three-year-old and his wife.

CHAPTER 3

Free Agency

Trying to win a fourth title in as many years would prove too much for the Shaq/Kobe Lakers. Injuries, new faces, and a slow start doomed the season. But that didn't stop Bryant from elevating his game to a new level, all while wearing some of the most sought-after sneakers of all time. Bryant played and started in all 82 games that season while averaging 41.5 minutes per game. Due to an increased role, he averaged 30 points, 5.9 assists, and 2.2 steals per game. Good enough to earn All-NBA First Team honors next to O'Neal and NBA All-Defensive First Team yet again.

The only thing more impressive than his eye-popping stats was what he had on his feet. During Bryant's sneaker free-agency season, he wore Jordan, Nike, Reebok, and AND1 sneakers.

Of the 82 games Bryant played in, he wore Air Jordan sneakers in 65 of those games. Multiple websites have made a herculean effort to document all of the sneakers Bryant wore during the season, most notably *Nice Kicks*[41] and *Sneaker Freaker*.[42] Here is the breakdown by model:

Air Jordan 3 PE
- Standard white leather with elephant print. Purple heel counter and gold Jumpman Logo
- Worn during eight games, including a 52-point game against the Rockets where he dunked on rookie Yao Ming

Air Jordan 3 "True Blue"
- General release colorway
- Worn in Atlanta during the 2003 NBA All-Star Game that was Michael Jordan's final All-Star Game

Air Jordan 6 Low "Chrome"
- General release colorway
- Worn once in Philadelphia against the 76ers where he scored 44 points

Air Jordan 7 PE
- Two pairs of PEs. A white colorway for home games, and a black colorway with a suede upper for road games
- Worn during eight games total. Three home games (including Christmas Day game debut), and five away games (including facing Jordan in Washington)

Air Jordan 8 PE
- White upper, purple tongue, and gold and gray accents on the midsole
- Worn during 16 games

Air Jordan 8 "Chrome"
- General release colorway
- Worn during 21 games

Air Jordan 11 "Concord"
- General release colorway
- Worn during three games, including season opener against the Spurs

Air Jordan 12 "Flint Grey"
- General release colorway
- Worn during one game against the SuperSonics

Air Jordan 12 "French Blue"
- General release colorway
- Worn during two games, both when the Lakers wore royal blue Hardwood Classics throwback uniforms

Air Jordan 17 "Black Metallic Silver"
- General release colorway
- Worn during three games, including duel with Tracy McGrady in Orlando

Air Jordan 17+ "Copper"
- General Release Colorway
- Worn during two games

Bryant's affinity for Jordan and his brand was apparent. However, he did rock a lot of other heat on the court that season. Here are the sneakers he wore from brands other than Jordan:

Nike Air Force 1 Mid PE
- White leather upper with gold Swoosh
- Worn during two games

Nike Air Max Elite
- White upper with silver Swoosh
- Worn during one game against the Warriors

Nike Air Flight Huarache PE
- White upper with purple and gold hints around the ankle and laces
- Worn during one game against the Raptors

Nike Zoom Turbine
- White upper with silver hints at midsole
- Worn during one game against the Bucks

Converse Weapon
- Lakers colorway, made famous by Magic Johnson
- Worn during one game against the Hawks

Reebok Question PE
- Five colorways (all black, white with purple toe, white with gold toe, white with silver toe)
- Worn during approximately five games
- The purple toe colorway was on his feet when he broke the NBA record for three-pointers made in a game against the SuperSonics

Reebok Answer IV PE
- White upper with purple overlay and gray midsole
- Worn during at least one game

AND1 Mid Desire
- All black colorway with silver hints
- Worn during one game against the Warriors

AND1 Game Time
- White upper with silver ankle collar and tongue
- Worn during one game against the Clippers

Just as it was difficult to defend Bryant, it was equally challenging to keep track of his footwear as he would sometimes switch sneakers at halftime. For 82 games that season, he tore the league up and set sneaker message boards ablaze.

Lakers Equipment Manager Rudy Garciduenas said he had his hands full during Bryant's sneaker free agency season. "I believe he felt stifled by the Adidas contract, and even with the creation of some of the weirdest shoes I'd ever seen, he still wasn't satisfied. He just was not satisfied with his ability to express himself. This period gave him the freedom to bounce his ideas off a lot of people and not be tied down."[43]

One of the heirs to Air Jordan, Jeffrey M. Jordan, was a kid at that time. He has since become an entrepreneur and head of digital innovation at Jordan Brand. When I asked what he remembered from the incredible season, Jordan said, "Besides a great season on the court,

I probably remember the commercials most. The marketing push seemed huge, especially during the playoffs in those early Millennium years."

Jordan continues, "I remember interning at Nike back in 2009, and the online sneaker community still buzzing about the sneaker free-agency period, which caught my attention at the time." Out of the 65 pairs of Air Jordan sneakers worn that season, Jordan called the Air Jordan 3 PE his personal favorite.[44]

Unfortunately for the Lakers, their dynasty was coming to a close. They defeated the No. 4-seed Timberwolves 4-2 in the first round of the playoffs before facing the Spurs in the second round. Despite the Lakers fighting back to tie the series after an 0-2 start, the Spurs narrowly won Game 5 in San Antonio and obliterated the defending champions in Game 6 in front of a stunned Staples Center crowd. It was the first series the team had lost since the Spurs swept them in the 1999 Western Conference Semifinals.

The championship streak was over. Since that time, no other NBA team has completed a three-peat. Coach Phil Jackson, Shaquille O'Neal, and Kobe Bryant all had one year remaining on their contracts. The organization would make a strong push in the summer of 2003 to surround their team's pillars with the help they needed.

What Ifs?

When Bryant left Adidas, it changed sneaker history. You could spend countless hours imagining what could have been different had he chosen to go in a different direction. So I conducted interviews with people of different backgrounds and industries throughout the summer of 2020 to get their opinion:

"I'm far from a shoe expert, but it's hard for me to imagine Kobe having as lasting and legendary a sneaker legacy with any brand other than Nike. That said, I think he potentially had the power and influence to forever change the way Adidas, Reebok, or any other sneaker brand is viewed in the basketball landscape." – Meredith Cash of *Business Insider*

"Speculating like this is always fun. Honestly, the only brand I could have seen Kobe with is Jordan Brand. The two athletes were so similar that it would have made sense to have had Kobe pick up the torch for MJ. But living in someone else's shadow was never really Kobe's thing. Kobe wasn't happy at Adidas and bought himself out of his contract. Reebok went downhill pretty quickly once Allen Iverson lost his mojo. Shawn Kemp never really worked out for them, and John Wall had the potential, but Reebok just didn't have any juice left. I feel Nike was the best fit for him. The Swoosh had the resources and personnel to create the shoes Kobe had envisioned. To create footwear that pushed the envelope and moved the needle forward in terms of innovation and what was possible with footwear at the time." – Chris Chase of WearTesters.com

"I honestly don't think his shoes would be as popular. We all saw what the second shoe Adidas made him look like, right? Plus, Nike's marketing is basically unmatched among other sneaker brands or most brands in general. Without question, I think his shoes are more popular with the Swoosh than they would have been elsewhere." – Harrison Faigen of *Silver Screen & Roll*

"Difficult to say, but Nike was the leader in progressive footwear, especially with NBA players. I'm not sure he would have been satisfied with anyone else." – Rudy Garciduenas former Lakers Equipment Manager

"Nike did wonders for Kobe's image and brand when he hit a rough period in his life. He wasn't satisfied with Adidas after the release of the Adidas Kobe 2 and felt that the brand was headed in a different direction design and performance-wise. I do wonder what would have happened if he went the Reebok route. Allen Iverson and Kobe were two of the most popular players of the 2000s, and it makes you think about what kind of impact that would have had on future players like LeBron James, who considered the brand before signing with Nike. Kobe was a huge star before he signed with Nike, but the brand certainly elevated him to global icon status." – Jarrel Harris of *Sports Illustrated*

"I can't say it would be the same legacy, but I can't say it would be any different either—the main reason being Kobe Bryant and everything that name means to the world. His magnetism and style were irrefutable. The way he approached the game on and off [the court] was unique—he had the vision of a 'creative' in the industry. And of course, the Mamba Mentality. I think any brand that would have had the chance to build and collaborate with Kobe would have benefited greatly." – Jeffrey M. Jordan of Jordan Brand and Jordan Avakian Group

"I don't think Kobe would have had the same sneaker legacy if he had stuck with Adidas. The brand opted for the 'team' format in the 2000s over giving players signature shoes, and the shoes they did give players were lackluster. Bryant and Nike designer Eric Avar were able to create a one-of-a-kind bond together and create truly innovative shoes that reflected Bryant's playing style, rather than gimmicks to market to the public." – Matt Welty of *Complex Sneakers*

"This question gives me a tough time to think about it. I feel like a player's signature legacy depends highly on his game. Like everyone wants Jordans. Jordan Brand became so strong. Their marketing is good, their product is good, everything is good. But all those are based on Michael Jordan being such a great player. Since Bryant was such a dynamic player, his sneaker legacy is still going to be good. If he had gone to another brand, he would still have had a signature line, and I think people would still have liked it." – Xinjie of @xinjie_sneakerseum

CHAPTER 4

The Swoosh

--- Nike ---

It was no secret Bryant had narrowed his decision down to Nike and Reebok during his sneaker free-agency season. Nike appeared to have the upper hand given Bryant's affinity for retro Jordans and Nike's newest technology. Reebok reportedly withdrew from the bidding war a week after the 2002 NBA All-Star Game, while Bryant claimed he walked away from them in negotiations.[45]

In June of 2003, Bryant officially signed a four-year contract with Nike for at least $40 million with royalties on a signature shoe that was in the works. Later it was clarified that he would wear Nike products, not Jordan Brand. Still, it was a far cry from the seven-year, $90-million contract that rookie LeBron James had just signed with the company.

In a 2003 article with the *Los Angeles Times*, Rick Burton, the executive director of the Warsaw Sports Marketing Center at the University of Oregon at the time, cast doubt on Bryant's ability to move sneakers. Burton said, "I don't know if we have any proof that Kobe's endorsement sells shoes. No disrespect to Kobe—he's a great guy—

but historically, if you look at what happened at Adidas, there's no proof of his ability [to sell shoes]." Burton continued, "Kobe could be justified in saying the product wasn't right, the marketing wasn't right, that it wasn't Kobe, it was the product. But if we take a historical perspective, we don't know that Kobe's name attached to a shoe will cause it to sell."[46]

Bryant wouldn't get his own signature model with the Swoosh until the third year of his contract. But that didn't stop the All-Star from teaming up with Nike designer Eric Avar to help create the Zoom Huarache 2K4, which he wore predominantly throughout the 2003-2004 season. The Huarache 2K4 was a superior performance model compared to what Bryant had been playing in previous seasons. The high-top sneaker had a synthetic leather upper with dotted perforations for ventilation, and a strap to help keep the ankle secure.

Nike went with a herringbone outsole and a carbon fiber plate under the forefoot to provide torsional support and spring.[47] One of the most noticeable things about this sneaker was the cushion. A large-volume Zoom Air unit was under the heel with a smaller Zoom Air unit under the ball of the foot. Unfortunately for fans, they had to wait until February of 2004 for Bryant to debut the new sneaker in Lakers home and away colorways. For the first half of the season, Bryant mixed in Nike Air Flight Huarache PEs and, surprisingly, Air Jordan 12s (Flint and French blue colorways), all of which he had worn the season prior.[48]

But before Bryant broke in his new sneakers, he would have to get comfortable with new teammates. During the offseason, veterans Karl Malone and Gary Payton took pay cuts to sign with the Lakers in hopes of winning a championship. The future Hall-of-Famers had the misfortune of playing at the same time as Michael Jordan and the Bulls. Malone had two finals losses, and Payton had one.

Even though the Lakers got off to a 14-3 start, the season was rife with turmoil. Coach Phil Jackson and perennial NBA Finals MVP Shaquille O'Neal quickly realized they would not be returning after the season. To further complicate matters, Malone and Payton had trouble finding rhythm throughout the season.

In Bryant's first matchup against the Cavaliers and rookie LeBron James on January 12, 2004, he laced up a pair of Nike Zoom Flight 2K3 in a white-and-gold colorway. Meanwhile, James, the future NBA Rookie of the Year, wore his first signature shoe—Nike Air

Zoom Generation in a black colorway with wine accents to match his Cavaliers uniform. While Bryant faced off-court problems, he turned in truly spectacular performances on the court. He started in 64 of the 65 games and led the team with 24 points and 1.7 steals per game. With the 2004 NBA All-Star Game held in Los Angeles, it was a no-brainer that Bryant and O'Neal would be the center of attention.

Bryant, who had received the most votes among Western Conference players, scored 20 points and received MVP chants from the home crowd. O'Neal, who was not voted a starter, would tally 24 points with 11 rebounds, which netted him the 2004 NBA All-Star Game Most Valuable Player Award. By this point in the season, Bryant wanted to dominate any player in his way. Night after night, he churned out highlight-reel plays with equally sensational Zoom Huarache 2K4 PEs on his feet.[49] Bryant closed out the regular season with an overtime win against the Trail Blazers that included two three-point buzzer-beaters.

His selection to both All-NBA First Team and NBA All-Defensive First Team were easy choices by media voters. Bryant led the Lakers to a 56-26 regular season record and a 2-seed in the Western Conference. The Rockets, Spurs, and eventually the 1-seed Timberwolves all got handled in a six-game series or less. But a gritty Pistons team was not to be denied. They were a defensive-minded team built perfectly for the Lakers. Chauncey Billups, Tayshaun Prince, Richard "Rip" Hamilton, Rasheed Wallace, and Ben Wallace were like the 2002 Kings but much tougher and lacked fear of the Lakers. The Pistons won the 2004 NBA Finals in a 4-1 gentleman's sweep.

After the season, the front office overhauled the team. Phil Jackson left, Gary Payton and Rick Fox were traded to the Celtics. Malone and Grant retired. Fisher signed with the Warriors, and O'Neal got traded to the Heat. To make matters worse for the Lakers, Bryant kept entertaining the thought of leaving the team during free agency. The Bulls, Clippers, Knicks, and Nuggets were all in contention. However, one day after the O'Neal trade, Bryant agreed to a seven-year, $136.4 million contract with the Lakers.[50] At the press conference held in the Lakers practice facility, Kobe had Vanessa by his side and his baby girl Natalia in his arms. He told the media he was happy to be a Laker for life.

Rebuild

It always had to be either Bryant or O'Neal. The expiration date on the two alphas coexisting had long passed. During the tumultuous 2003-2004 season, Bryant reinvented himself as he would do throughout his career. Now with a tattooed tribute to his family on his arm, he was bulkier and tougher than ever. In fact, he'd created an alter ego. Bryant dubbed himself "the Black Mamba."[51]

The black mamba is a venomous snake that strikes with 99% accuracy at maximum speed in rapid succession. The serpent was featured in the 2004 Quentin Tarantino movie *Kill Bill: Volume 2*. Bryant needed the killer mindset if he was going to drag the roster he had through the season. The Lakers went 34-48 missing the playoffs, and new coach Rudy Tomjanovich was replaced by Frank Hamblen in February of 2004 due to health problems.

Fans again voted for Bryant to start in the NBA All-Star Game thanks to an average of 27.6 points and six assists per game. However, the media only named him to the All-NBA Third Team. In retrospect, the media soured on Bryant by the mid-2000s, and it would take years for them to come back around.

Despite the losing season, Bryant continued to forge his sneaker legacy. He began the season in the Huarache 2K4 with a slew of PEs in Lakers colorways.[52] The infamous "baptism" where Bryant dunked on rookie Dwight Howard clearly shows a pair of all-black Huarache 2K4s on feet. On Christmas Day, the Lakers faced off against the Heat for the first time since the O'Neal trade. It was the perfect time and place to debut the Nike Air Zoom Huarache 2K5 in a crispy white and purple colorway. Again, designed by Eric Avar, the Huarache 2K5 built on the foundation of its predecessor.

The new model kept heel and forefoot Zoom Air cushioning, along with a carbon fiber plate and ankle strap for additional stability. In an era of heavy high-tops, the Huarache 2K5 only weighed 14.4 ounces.[53] But most importantly, it was the first basketball sneaker to use Nike Free technology. The idea for Nike Free came from Stanford University, where Nike designers saw runners ending their workouts by running barefoot on grass. The coach believed it to be good for foot health. Nike essentially put slices in the outsole of shoes for more flexibility to replicate the natural barefoot motion.[54] The technological breakthrough was here to stay.

The tooling for the Huarache 2K5 was sound, while the appearance made the sneaker stand out from the crowd. The new upper, inspired by samurai warriors, came in a plethora of PE colorways for Bryant. The #8 stitched across the strap served as the cherry on top of an already timeless sneaker.

2005-2006

On June 14, 2005, the Lakers signed Phil Jackson to serve as the head coach for another three years. To the surprise of many, Jackson, Bryant, and the Lakers front office were all able to reconcile their past differences. In his time away from the team, Jackson wrote a book in 2004 titled *The Last Season: A Team in Search of Its Soul*. In the book, Jackson gave his account of the 2003-2004 season and was markedly critical of Bryant as a player.[55]

With the Hall of Fame coach in his corner, Bryant proceeded to rip up the league. Albeit a league dressed differently. For most of the previous decade, Allen Iverson was the fashion trendsetter for the league. That meant baggy pants, oversized jerseys, and expensive jewelry. Under the new dress code policy implemented by Commissioner David Stern, players had to maintain a more business-casual approach. Slacks, a dress shirt, and a suit coat would be the new normal. There could be no sneakers, sunglasses, or chains worn.[56] That meant no more Philadelphia Eagles jerseys for Bryant when he wasn't playing.

Dress code drama aside, Bryant put together one of the most impressive offensive seasons the league had ever seen. He started his tour de force in the Huarache 2K5 in a special home and away colorway. Both the black-and-white PEs had a new snakeskin graphic lasered on the upper.[57] The Huarache 2K5 is the first Nike sneaker to feature the Kobe logo known as the Sheath. The logo consists of six different shapes. Combined together, they form a geometric shape similar to a tricorn, or the sheath of a samurai sword.

In a 2007 interview with *Esquire*, Bryant explained the sword to be "raw talent," while the sheath, which packages the sword, represents "everything you go through, your calluses and your baggage, what you learn."[58] In a scene from Quentin Tarantino's 2003 movie *Kill Bill: Volume 1*, Uma Thurman's character The Bride has a similar logo on her sword.[59] It's safe to assume that Bryant was a fan of the film series.

To further hype up the sneaker, a special city streets series released in limited quantities in select cities. Nike printed maps of Los Angeles and Boston on the upper in rare Lakers and Celtics colorways, which quickly sold out.[60] On December 20, 2005, Bryant had the home PE on his feet during his 62-point game against the Mavericks. The clinic he put on that night was just one of the five games he scored more than 50 points in a game that season.

Bryant and the Zoom Huarache line will forever be linked together in sneaker history. There would be many more occasions where Bryant returned to the model. But something much bigger was about to take place.

CHAPTER 5

Black Mamba

Nike Zoom Kobe 1

Less than a week after the 62-point game against the Mavericks, Bryant debuted his first signature sneaker with Nike. On Christmas Day 2005, the Lakers traveled to Miami to take on the Heat. Even though Bryant scored 37 points, the Heat won the game 97-92. Former Lakers O'Neal and Payton combined for 39 points, while Dwyane Wade chipped in another 18 points. The outcome of the regular season matchup was no surprise, but the debut of the Nike Zoom Kobe 1 in a black-and-gold colorway (known as the Del Sol colorway) is what excited diehard sneakerheads.

Designed by Kevin Link and Kobe Bryant, the Kobe 1 was both stylish and cutting edge. The sneaker used a leather upper, including a strip over the tongue featuring the Kobe logo, and a large Swoosh on both the medial and lateral sides of the upper. But the materials Nike used were what set the Kobe 1 apart from the field. A thick rubber outsole with herringbone and diamond traction patterns provided adequate traction. The Nike Swoosh on the bottom of the sneaker revealed a portion of a nearly full-length carbon fiber plate.[61] Additional support was provided by keeping the outsole flat and wide, complete with outriggers to help prevent injuries.

For the cushion, individual Zoom Air units were placed in the heel and under the ball of the foot. Foam padding around the inside of the sneaker, including the tongue, helped complete the comfortable experience. A foam collar with mesh overlays wrapped around the ankle, excluding a small portion near the back of the ankle meant to provide mobility. One noticeable sign of the times was the "Uptempo" branding across the back of the heel. Nike used to have a specific series of sneakers designed for certain player archetypes. Flight, Force, and Uptempo were used to designate which model was best for your style.[62] The Uptempo line had included forwards like Scottie Pippen and Charles Barkley. Whereas Flight catered to smaller guards and Force was built for more powerful post players.

The design and materials used in the Kobe 1 lent itself to some very memorable colorways. Lakers Equipment Manager Rudy Garciduenas recalls, "The Kobe 1 was still a traditional basketball styling (3/4 to high), but he had fun with the colorways."[63] A Lakers home colorway become historic on the night of January 22, 2006. What started as a slow scoring night turned into the second-highest, single-game performance in NBA history.

After 26 points at halftime, Bryant erupted for 55 additional points in the second half of a comeback victory against the Raptors. The 81-point performance in front of a raucous home crowd was one of the most mesmerizing games in Bryant's career. Only Wilt Chamberlain, who scored 100 points in a game, sat ahead of him in the record books. On Bryant's feet were the Kobe 1s in a simple Lakers home colorway. White leather, black Swoosh, and a purple ankle collar. The colorway was dubbed the "81-point PE" and quickly became one of the most important sneakers in Bryant's time with Nike. Fun fact: a year later Nike released 81 pairs of the PE in size 14 to commemorate the historic accomplishment. Fans had to search around Downtown Los Angeles in a scavenger hunt to find the sneakers.[64]

The Kobe 1 and Kobe's signature clothing line went on sale nationwide just over a week before the 2006 NBA All-Star Game. After the first half of the season Bryant put together, he was a shoo-in to start in the 2006 NBA All-Star Game held in Houston. Bryant surprisingly only scored eight points in the exhibition but did break out the Kobe 1 in a red, white, and blue "All-Star" colorway designed to match the Western Conference uniforms.

Nike's first commercial that featured the Kobe 1 was straight forward and true to Bryant's real personality. His prodigious work ethic was well known, so the commercial featured Bryant working out.[65] Bryant narrated the commercial as the clips of him lifting weights and practicing moves on the court rolled.

> *Love me or hate me, it's one or the other—always has been.*
> *Hate my game, my swagger. Hate my fadeaway, my hunger.*
> *Hate that I'm a veteran, a champion. Hate that.*
> *Hate it with all of your heart.*
> *Hate that I'm loved for the exact same reasons.*

The debut commercial was both honest and inspiring. Bryant and Nike were a match made in heaven. It was his idea for them to film his workouts and turn it into a commercial. He had learned his lessons from the past, and Nike enabled his creative genius to flourish in plain view.

The 2005-2006 season had some incredible highs for Bryant. His season-long attack on the league earned him All-NBA First Team and NBA All-Defensive First Team honors. Nike released his new signature sneaker and clothing line, plus he had the fourth-highest jersey sales that season. Unfortunately for Bryant and the Lakers, the season ended on a bitter note. A 45-37 regular season record meant the Lakers would have to face the 2-seed Suns in the first round of the Western Conference playoffs.

In Game 4 of the series, Bryant hit a layup at the buzzer to force overtime. In overtime, Bryant sank a 15-footer over two Suns defenders as time expired to win the game. The excitement of the Staples Center crowd was only exceeded by Bryant's teammates who mobbed him during the post-game celebration. Of course, the Kobe 1 PEs that Bryant wore on his feet would take on a life of their own. The "Final Seconds" colorway, as they became known, featured white leather, a gold Swoosh, and both a purple collar and outsole.

After the pair of buzzer beaters, hoopers everywhere at every level imitated Bryant's postgame celebration. Left arm out with the fist clenched with an absolutely determined look. Then moments later, grabbing the jersey with the left hand and pulling it across the chest.[66]

On May 1, 2006, something far more important than any shot, win, or sneaker took place. Kobe and Vanessa's second daughter, Gianna, was born. For as competitive as Bryant was on the court, his family was always the most important thing in his life.

The Lakers soon learned that a 3-1 series lead against Steve Nash and the Suns is never safe. The Lakers let games 5, 6, and 7 slip away. In Game 7, Bryant had 23 points in the first half and only a single point in the second half. His frustration with his teammates in the 121-90 blowout was palpable. To make matters worse, the Miami Heat won the 2006 NBA Finals against the Dallas Mavericks in a 4-2 series. Payton got his first ring while O'Neal got the all-critical fourth ring of his career. The championship with the Heat proved that O'Neal could win without Bryant. At the time, it vindicated his move to Miami. The ball was now in Bryant's court to catch up with O'Neal. For better and for worse, the following season would serve as déjà vu for Kobe Bryant and the Lakers.

Nike Zoom Kobe II

By the spring of 2006, news broke that Bryant was changing his number from 8 to 24. Many fans immediately speculated that it had something to do with symbolically passing up Michael Jordan, who wore number 23. But the answer was much more complicated.

Bryant started his high school career wearing number 24 before switching to number 33. Kobe's father Joe had worn number 33 in high school as well. However, Kobe could not wear number 33 after being traded to the Lakers since that number was hanging in the rafters thanks to Kareem Abdul-Jabbar.

So, he landed on the number 8 for two reasons. First, it was the number he wore in Italy as a kid. Second, he added up his number (143) from the Adidas ABCD camp. But why the change to number 24 now? Bryant wanted a clean slate after the O'Neal trade. But he had to wait another season due to a league-mandated deadline on changing jersey numbers. In a 2017 interview with Baxter Holmes of ESPN Bryant gave the following answer:

"Then 24 is a growth from that. Physical attributes aren't there the way they used to be, but the maturity level is greater. Marriage, kids. Start having a broader perspective being one of the older guys on the team now as opposed to being the youngest. Things evolve. It's not to say one is better than the other or one's a better way to be. It's just growth."

Bryant continued to say, "It's a new book, 24—24 is *every day*. Because when you get older, your muscles start getting sore. Body starts aching. You show up to practice that day, you have to remind yourself, 'OK, this day is the most important day. I got to push through this soreness. My ankles are tight, they won't get loose. I got to go through it, because this is the most important day.' So, 24 also helped me from a motivational standpoint."[67]

Over the course of just a few years, Bryant successfully reinvented himself. Short hair, tattoos, new agent, new sneaker company, and no more playing second fiddle to another teammate. The transformation from a spirited showboat to a surly serpent was complete. Throughout the 2006-2007 season, Bryant made the league pay for his unceremonious playoff exit the prior spring. Starting in all 77 games in which he played, Bryant averaged 31.6 points, 5.4 assists, and 1.4 steals per game.

Bryant started the season wearing the Kobe 1 in new Lakers colorways, which played with new color-blocking schemes. But like the previous season before, he debuted the Nike Zoom Kobe II on Christmas Day 2006.[68] In retrospect, it wasn't the best game to debut the Kobe 2. The Heat trounced the Lakers 101-85, while Dwyane Wade outscored Bryant 40 to 16.

Nevertheless, the Kobe 2 was an important step in Bryant's signature sneaker line with Nike. The model came in three different styles known as the "Weapons of War." The Sheath, Strength, and Lite versions. The main difference between the three sneakers was the straps. The Sheath featured one strap across the ankle, the Strength featured a strap over the ankle and midfoot, while the Lite had no straps.[69]

Bryant (and fans) seem to prefer the less-flashy Sheath version. The Kobe 2 featured a leather upper and leather strap that read "KOBE" across the front and "24" on the side. The leather was segmented by ventilation holes, which wrapped around the back half of the shoe. Over the diamond perforations sat a large Swoosh, while the Kobe logo took up most of the sneaker's rear.

The visual appeal for the Kobe 2 was adequate, but the tooling is what set it apart from other sneakers at the time.

The design team again incorporated Nike Free technology on the outsole which segmented divided pods of rubber herringbone traction. In the middle of the outsole, a carbon fiber plate was used with "2" on the left foot and "4" on the right foot. The Kobe 2 was noticeably less wide and flatter than its predecessor. For cushion, the Kobe 2 featured a sewn-in Zoom insole. The interior was heavily padded with extra foam with a mesh overlay added to hug the Achilles tendon. Besides making the sneaker more comfortable, it helped keep the foot locked into place.

Nike's second commercial featuring Bryant was more avant garde. A black screen with parallel images mirrored each other on opposite sides of the screen. Starting with Bryant's face, to him dribbling the ball, to the Kobe 2, then Bryant dunking, before a single image of Bryant staring at the camera with his arms folded. The commercial ends with abstract shapes swirling around the screen to eventually form the Kobe logo with the words "Zoom Kobe II" finally appearing.[70]

Over the artsy images, Bryant narrates the commercial in what sounds like a fuzzy voice recording left on a cell phone.

> *With me, you kind of push the boundaries a little bit.*
> *I understand that, you know, to try to get that next level you have to take risks.*
> *I mean, this is what helps you be the best basketball player you can be, you know?*
> *That's why, you know, we focus on it from the beginning all the way to the end.*

Nike rolled out the three versions of the Kobe 2 over the course over several months. The Sheath released on April 1, 2007. The Strength was released a month later on May 1, 2007. Meanwhile, the Lite would have to wait six months before being released in October 2007.[71] Despite an interesting look and experimentation with new ideas, the Kobe 2 never enjoyed the same popularity of other models from the Nike Kobe sneaker line. However, that didn't stop Bryant from wreaking havoc in the sneaker.

At the 2007 NBA All-Star Game held in Las Vegas, Bryant debuted a colorway that demanded the attention of sneakerheads. A white upper with a gold Swoosh and tongue, complemented by a red strap and midsole. The PE matched the Sin City-themed uniforms to a T. The Western Conference blew out the Eastern Conference 153-132, thanks to Bryant's 31-point performance. Bryant snagged his second NBA All-Star Game Most Valuable Player Award, and this time no fans booed him.

If the league thought the All-Star performance would quench the Black Mamba's thirst for blood, they soon received a rude awakening. In March of 2007, Bryant somehow took his game up another level. Four straight games with over 50 points, all of which resulted in wins for the Lakers. Beginning March 16, Bryant scored 65 points against the Trail Blazers. Two days later, he dropped 50 points against the Timberwolves. Four days later, he poured in 60 points on the road against the Grizzlies. The very next night, another 50-piece for the Hornets in New Orleans.

Just for good measure, he gave another 43-point performance against the Warriors once the Lakers returned home on March 25. Of the ten remaining regular season games, Bryant scored over 46 points in three of the matchups. The man was a problem for the league. Love or hate the Nike Zoom Kobe 2, Bryant might have been at the top of his offensive game when he laced them up. The media mercifully voted him to be All-NBA First Team and NBA All-Defensive First Team yet again. Plus, his 31.6 points per game made him the NBA scoring champion.

But much like the season prior, his team wasn't ready to take the next step in the playoffs. A mediocre 42-40 regular season record barely got them into the playoffs as the 7-seed. Ironically, they had the same record as the "We Believe" Warriors who went on to upset the 1-seed Mavericks in the first round of the Western Conference playoffs. The Lakers would not be as fortunate. Steve Nash and the Suns eliminated the Lakers for the second straight year, this time in a 4-1 gentleman's sweep. It would be the last time the Lakers got embarrassed in the playoffs for several years to come.

Not long after the season ended, Bryant voiced his displeasure with the front office for the roster they had assembled. The tension between the two parties boiled over the summer, so much so the front office negotiated trade proposals with both the Pistons and Bulls, respectively.[72] Eventually, cooler heads prevailed, and Bryant remained in Los Angeles.

From 2002-2006, the USA Basketball Men's National team suffered several embarrassing losses on the international stage. Luckily, Bryant and several other NBA All-Stars would participate in the 2007 FIBA Americas Championship. The United States won a 118-81 Finals victory over Argentina in Las Vegas. On Bryant's feet were the Kobe 2s in a clean, USA colorway. On his chest, the number 10. Yes, more speculation about jersey numbers. It's worth noting that Michael Jordan wore the number 9 when he played on the Dream Team in the 1992 Olympics in Barcelona. Was Bryant trying to one-up Jordan with a jersey number again?

No, actually, the reason was more intriguing than something that trivial. Growing up in Italy, Bryant played a lot of soccer. His affinity for the game carried well into adulthood. In soccer, the number 10 is for the team's striker or playmaker.[73] Bryant would be the go-to guy for the 2007 Men's National Team and would play an even larger role in the Beijing Olympics the following summer.

Late in the summer of 2007, posters of Bryant in the Kobe 2 with a pair of gigantic wings attached to his back surfaced online. To the left of Bryant read:

> *ZOOM KOBE II*
> *SUPERNATURAL*
> *(Bryant's signature)*
> *I'm chasing perfection. Elevating my game.*
> *Zoom Kobe II helps me be the best player I can be.*
> *Natural fit and motion. Supernatural performance.*
> *NIKEBASKETBALL.COM*

It was the promotional poster for the "Kobe Bryant SUPERNATURAL Asian Tour September 2007 by Nike." Building on his international popularity, Bryant visited five important cities. Manilla on September 5, Taipei on September 6, Hong Kong on September 7, Shanghai on September 8, and Beijing on September 9 and 10.[74]

As part of the tour, Bryant held basketball clinics for kids of all ages. Thousands of fans packed the streets to get a glimpse of the reigning NBA scoring champion. Their excitement was matched only by Bryant himself. He worked his way through the crowd, giving high fives and smiling ear-to-ear for pictures with fans.

—— More Huaraches, Nike Kobe III, Hyperdunks ——

The Lakers celebrated their 60th anniversary throughout the 2007-2008 season, and it was a year to remember. A series of savvy roster moves helped surround Bryant with the help he needed. Free agent Derek Fisher was brought back into the fold. Then in November, the Lakers traded for Trevor Ariza. Additionally, Lamar Odom and Sasha Vujacic were coming of age. Thanks to hard work and being pushed by Coach Jackson and Bryant every day, they were starting to reach their full potential.

At age 29, Bryant started all 82 games of the regular season, while averaging 38.9 minutes per game. Oddly enough, he didn't start the season in the Kobe 2. Bryant laced up a shiny new pair of Huarache 2K4s coated in patent leather.[75] The reason for the switch-up might have had more to do with Nike than Bryant. In 2004, the Huarache 2K4 with laser print designs on the upper was an Asia exclusive. Three years later, they released in the United States.[76] So, Bryant, the ambassador of the Huarache line, laced up several pairs of home and away PEs at the beginning of the season.

Breaking with tradition, Bryant debuted the Nike Zoom Kobe III a few days before Christmas.[77] On December 20, 2007, the Lakers lost a tough road matchup against LeBron James and the Cavaliers. But that didn't stop Bryant from scoring 21 points with an all-black pair of his newest sneakers on his feet.

The Kobe 3 looked radically different than the previous two models. Designed by Eric Avar and Kobe Bryant, the sneaker's most noticeable feature was the upper. Besides a leather toe cap, the entire upper was wrapped in a scale design—or waffle pattern, or diamond pattern, depending on who you ask. Some have suggested it is a diamond pattern inspired by Bryant's oldest daughter, Natalia Diamante Bryant.

Directly underneath the rubber upper, a urethane mesh. The Swoosh logo took a backseat and sat on the heel. In contrast, the Kobe logo resided on the tongue. Laces ran up to the top of the ankle (a feature that would change in the coming years). The sneaker offered adequate cushioning with Zoom Air under the heel and forefoot.[78] The outsole was flat with a carbon fiber plate and sturdy outrigger for extra support. Instead of herringbone, the designers implemented a diamond pattern design to aid in traction.[79] Thanks to materials used in the Kobe 3, it was a breathable and light sneaker that could be enjoyed by outdoor hoopers as well.

Two days after debuting the Kobe 3 in Cleveland, Bryant attended a Nike event at the House of Hoops in Harlem to promote the new sneaker.[80] The following night Bryant scored 39 points in a win against the Knicks. He became the youngest player to score 20,000 career points. Naturally, Bryant looked over to taunt Spike Lee, who sat courtside in Madison Square Garden that night. The next week, Bryant wore an exquisite PE on December 30 against the Celtics. The PE featured a purple upper with a white diamond pattern and Swoosh. The midsole and ankle collar had hints of gold.

The only thing off about the look didn't involve the sneakers at all. The team wore short-shorts in the first half of the game. The short-shorts meant to pay homage to the Showtime-era Lakers, but the 2007 squad changed back into their normal shorts at halftime. The Celtics won 110-91, and the short-shorts were retired for good.[81]

As Bryant's sneaker line matured, so did Nike's marketing of the eclectic star athlete. Three commercials promoted the Kobe 3.[82] The first features a young kid holding the sneaker while asking what if Mozart only had half the notes to compose with, while Bryant sits in the background facing away from the camera, dressed in proper 18th-century attire. The kid proclaims that "genius needs a full range to explore." He holds up the Kobe 3 and says the sneakers played every note on the scale—by this time, Bryant is throwing down dunks and sinking jump shots in the background. The commercial ends with the kid saying, "We're not born geniuses. We become them."

The second commercial took a more traditional and less comical angle. Against a dark backdrop, Bryant moves through defenders in slow motion while weighing strengths and weaknesses (which appeared in video-game-style graphics).

Bryant narrated the commercial:

> *Look deeper.*
> *I am more than just dunks and fadeaways.*
> *You see what I see? The angles, inches, and split seconds?*
> *The miles I ran, the weights I lifted.*
> *The options, the counters.*

See the game one move ahead. That's where you'll find me.
Digging in just a little deeper. To rise above and beyond.

On February 1, 2008, the Lakers got the final piece of the puzzle needed to become championship contenders—Pau Gasol. It cost the team a slew of young players and draft picks (including his younger brother, Marc Gasol). Gasol and Bryant quickly hit it off. Not only did they speak Spanish with each other on the court, they seemed to be able to communicate telepathically. One could nod or blink, and the other would cut in the perfect direction to complete the play. The two friends grew to be more like brothers or *hermanos*, as they regularly said throughout the years.

Two weeks after the Gasol trade, Bryant started in the 2008 NBA All-Star Game in New Orleans. The gold-and-red "All Star" colorway of the Kobe 3s he wore were made available to the public in very limited supply. It was apparent Nike and Bryant were starting to have more fun in the creative process. Colorways began taking on a storytelling role, such as the MPLS (blue and gray), Lower Merion Aces (maroon and silver), Asia (black and gold),[83] and the exclusive Lakers colorway (gray, purple, and gold) which only released in Asia and Kobe events hosted at House of Hoops locations in the United States.[84]

Lakers Equipment Manager Rudy Garciduenas was busier than ever. "Kobe would always be shipped a sizeable amount to the Lakers. If there was anything special or prototypes, then Nico [Harrison] (a Nike representative) would walk in with a few pairs, and if he liked them, Nico and I would arrange shipping quantity later."[85]

By April of 2008, Bryant had packed more memorable moments into a season than most players do in a career. But he wasn't even close to being finished—including debuting more sneakers. Bryant eventually became the face of the Nike Hyerpdunk.

Designer Eric Avar had been experimenting in the Nike Innovation Kitchen for two years on this model. The two most important innovations involved support and cushion. For the first time, Nike implemented Flywire technology to help keep the foot locked into place. Inspired by cables used in bridge designs, Jay Meschter, Innovation Director of Nike's Innovation Kitchen, discovered shoes could be more supportive with the use of long Vectran strands that wrap around the medial and lateral sides of the foot.

Meanwhile, Nike worked with NASA engineers to create a new cushion called Lunar Foam. Nike mixed EVA with nitrate rubber, which resulted in a springy foam that weighed 30% less than Phylon (cushion that had been used for the past decade).[86] The design team kept a large-volume Zoom Air unit in the heel, while the forefoot utilized the Lunar Foam for a springy step.

The major advancements in technology resulted in the lightest basketball sneaker ever created by Nike—13 ounces (men's size 9). The performance was the most important factor, but it did not hurt that the sneaker looked cool too. Thin panels of polyurethane with visible Flywire constituted the upper, with a large Swoosh over on top. A noticeably large midsole and heel cup aided in lockdown, while the laces helped keep the midfoot and ankle working in unison rather than a detached and unstable feeling.

The solid rubber outsole had a few distinct features—solid blocking throughout the outsole, except for the forefoot grooves. And a circle of herringbone with a Swoosh at the pivot point. The heel and forefoot of the outsole are decoupled with a sculpted carbon fiber plate to add torsional support and a more natural stepping motion.

The 2008 Olympics in Beijing served as the official coming-out party for the Nike Hyperdunk. But Nike and Bryant couldn't wait to try them out. So, Nike put a Kobe Logo on the tongue and let Bryant work his magic in the space-age sneakers. Marketing for the Hyperdunks was pure brilliance. Nike had a plan to capitalize on the emergence of YouTube, social media, and viral videos. In what appeared to be an amateur video, Bryant is setting up a camera and displays the Hyperdunks in a black-and-purple colorway. He warns watchers, "Do not try what I'm about to attempt right now."

Teammate Ronnie Turiaf stands by nervously, trying to talk Bryant out of whatever he's about to do. Bryant slides on the sneakers as he assures Turiaf that he's got this. Bryant, in a black Nike jumpsuit, walks away from the camera and gestures to someone. "Come on, bring it down." Seconds later, an Aston Martin DB9 Volante drop-top comes flying through the screen. Bryant easily leaps over the luxury vehicle. Bryant and Turiaf howl with excitement as they chest bump and celebrate the daring feat.

Bryant puts his face in the camera and says, "That is how you jump over an Aston Martin, boy! That's how you do it. Hyperdunks! Do not try this at home." The grainy video circulated around the world within hours.[87] It spawned spoof attempts, but more importantly, it put Hyperdunks on the map. One of the spoofs included Bryant himself. On the MTV show *Jackass*, Bryant appeared to jump over a 20-foot pool filled with snakes and finish with an outrageous dunk. The video was clearly edited, but it poured gasoline on an already burning viral sensation.

In the penultimate game of the regular season, Bryant wore a pair of Hyperdunks against the Spurs. The Lakers colorway featured purple patent leather that absolutely glistened on camera. Bryant scored 20 points in a 106-85 blowout. To make matters better, the Spurs game was filmed by 30 different cameras as part of Spike Lee's documentary *Kobe Doin' Work*. To add more access, Bryant wore a microphone throughout the game. ESPN aired the documentary thirteen months later.

Bryant was the star of the biggest sneaker marketing campaign of the new century. The sneakers, the viral videos, the newness of social media. It's a moment locked in time—an important chapter in sneaker history. The Hyperdunks will forever be synonymous with Bryant. But sneakers aside, Bryant's 2007-2008 season was one for the ages. Bryant started in all 82 games, averaging 28.3 points, 5.4 assists, and 1.84 steals per game in 38.9 minutes. He led the Lakers in all four categories. Thanks to his herculean effort, the Lakers were 57-25 and the 1-seed in the Western Conference Playoffs.

Bryant's slash-and-burn campaign netted him the 2008 NBA Most Valuable Player Award. Despite accruing statistics that matched and often exceeded his contemporaries, he had never won the award until now. After sweeping the Nuggets in the first round, Bryant lifted the trophy in front of the Staples Center crowd during the Western Conference Semifinals against the Jazz. After a 4-2 series victory against the Jazz, the Lakers faced the 3-seed Spurs. The Lakers only dropped one game in San Antonio, en route to a 4-1 gentleman's sweep. Bryant averaged 29.2 points per game in the Western Conference Finals.

After several years of trying, the Lakers had finally clawed their way back to the NBA Finals. Waiting for them was the "Boston Big 3." Led by Kevin Garnett, Ray Allen, and Paul Pierce, the Celtics were a gritty team. A 66-16 regular seed had earned the Celtics the

1-seed. However, it took two seven-game series and a six-game series to clinch the Eastern Conference Championship. Nevertheless, the league's most storied franchises met again in the NBA Finals to add another chapter to the history books.

Suited up in Kobe 3 PEs in Lakers colorways, Bryant took it to the Celtics in every game. The newly crowned MVP averaged 25.7 points and five assists per game in 43 minutes. But Bryant's effort wasn't enough to stop Boston's Big 3. The Celtics took the series in six games, including a 39-point shellacking in front of a ravenous home crowd. After congratulating his opponents, Bryant walked off the court in disgust as green confetti flew through the air. Years later, Bryant revealed that he listened to the songs from Journey and Dropkick Murphys that were played relentlessly in Boston. Until he got a rematch with the Celtics in 2010 NBA Finals, he forced himself to listen to the music that drove him crazy in 2008.[88]

After playing in the 2007 FIBA Americas Championship, starting 82 games and 21 playoff games, most players would be down for the count. But Bryant still had more to prove, and Nike was by his side to help him do it. On June 28, Nike released in very limited quantities the Nike Kobe 3 MVP Edition Pack. The simple colorway featured a white upper, gold stripe along the midsole, and purple Swoosh. The sneakers came in a special lasered acrylic box with an MVP shirt. Unfortunately for most fans, the release was limited to a few Asian countries and some lucky retailers in Los Angeles.

The next week, Bryant would continue his viral marketing campaign of the Hyperdunks. Based on the movie *Back to the Future*, Nike designed a special "Marty McFly" colorway. Only 350 pairs were made, with 100 of them going to the boutique store Undefeated (UNDFTD) located in Santa Monica. To add fuel to the fire, Bryant rolled up in a DeLorean. The first ten people in line got to meet the superstar and get his autograph on the ultra-rare pair of kicks.[89] A month later, Bryant was on a plane to China for the 2008 Summer Olympics.

CHAPTER 6

Ringsssss

Loaded with NBA All-Stars like Kobe Bryant, LeBron James, Dwyane Wade, and Carmelo Anthony, this iteration of Team USA was dubbed the "Redeem Team." The nickname played off the 1992 team's moniker of "Dream Team" and acknowledged the shortcomings of previous teams on the international stage.

Despite being heavy favorites, the tournament was far from a coronation for Team USA. In the Gold Medal Game against Spain, the Gasol brothers and Ricky Rubio hung around well into the fourth quarter. Bryant took over late to win 118-107 and secure his first gold medal. It was another important milestone in Bryant's career. Nike made sure to have a special Hyperdunk PE that featured a snakeskin design around the toe and ankle collar for the special moment.[90] Less than two months later, the Lakers tipped off the 2008-2009 season. Bryant had been on a non-stop whirlwind tour for the past two years. The Beatles would have scoffed at the schedule he maintained during this period.

Kobe IV

Now more than ever, Bryant needed sneakers that were light and supportive. He continued to wear the Hyperdunks at the beginning of the season before breaking the mold of what a basketball sneaker could be on December 19, 2008. In a nationally televised matchup against the Heat in Miami, Bryant debuted the Nike Zoom Kobe IV. In a special segment of the telecast, Nancy Lieberman of ESPN held up a pair of Kobe 4s in a black-and-purple colorway. To her (and many others') amazement, it was a low-top sneaker. She cited Steve Nash and Gilbert Arenas having previously worn low-top sneakers, but this was a first in the Nike Kobe signature line.

Designer Eric Avar kept the upper on the Kobe 4 similar to the Hyperdunks. Visible flywire encased in polyurethane panels on the midfoot with synthetic leather on the toe cap. Naturally, a sizable Swoosh logo was on both sides of the foot, with the Kobe Logo on the tongue. Speckled laces ran up a breathable mesh tongue (with the exception of the top of the tongue). A TPU heel counter was what kept the foot in place and prevented ankle injuries. The Kobe 4 debunked the myth that sneakers needed leather and lacing to run high up the ankle to protect against injuries. For extra branding, the number 24 was imprinted above the heel counter.

Traction was top of the line thanks to a soft rubber outsole that used a herringbone pattern in a splatter design. Two different-colored portions of the outsole made for a unique look. The flat outsole of previous Kobe models was gone. A carbon fiber plate helped bridge the heel to the forefoot, while a lateral outrigger further protected ankles from turning over. For the cushion, Nike used a phylon midsole with a Zoom Air unit in the heel.[91] The interior was heavily padded, which hugged the foot for extra comfort.

Chris Chase of WearTesters.com turned an interest in sneakers into something of an empire. Chase started breaking down the technical aspects of sneakers on YouTube more than a decade ago and now has well over half a million subscribers in addition to a popular website and social media accounts. Few, if any, people are more respected when it comes to giving their opinion on performance basketball footwear. We exchanged emails during June of 2020 for this book.

Chase points to the Kobe 4 as the most important sneaker in Kobe's signature sneaker line. "It broke the mold as far as what basketball players thought they could wear in a game. Additionally, it finally forced brands to omit false advertisements from years past, claiming high-tops offered more ankle support. When, in fact, ankle support doesn't come from the height of the shoe's collar at all. That only limited mobility and offered ankle restriction versus support."

He continued, "True support comes from ensuring the shoe fits as one-to-one as possible and by keeping the foot on top of the footbed via proper fit, lockdown, and with the aid of a proper heel counter."

Chase recalled, "Kobe mentioned in press marketing that he was inspired by the minimalistic approach to futbol boots (soccer cleats for Americans). Every player wore ultra-low-cut cleats and made similar lateral movements to basketball players, yet rarely encountered ankle injuries. Thus, the low cut became more popular than it had in its controversial past."[92]

Family friend and *SLAM* Magazine contributor Anthony Gilbert conducted an exclusive interview with Bryant shortly after the release of the Kobe 4. Gilbert recalled, "He was so knowledgeable about the sneaker industry and the 18-month-long process of making shoes. He knew exactly what he wanted, and he prided himself on always being different and accomplishing as much as he could at a young age."

Gilbert, a Philadelphia-native who had been in attendance for the 2002 NBA All-Star Game, added important context. "He wasn't the most-liked athlete in Philadelphia, yet when the Nike Kobe IV came out, the low-cut shoes looked so good that they had mass appeal outside of the game, and even the people who couldn't stand him bought his shoes and warmed up to the idea of supporting him."[93]

On Christmas Day 2008, the Lakers snapped the Celtics' 19-game winning streak. Bryant wore a Kobe 4 PE, which featured a predominantly gold upper sans the white side panels and purple Swoosh. The red laces added a festive spirit to the new sneaker. Luckily for a select few fans, Nike was in a giving mood. One hundred fans at the Staples Center got a pair of Kobe 4s in a white, purple, and red colorway, packaged in a red gym bag.[94] Meanwhile, the new sneaker was made available for customization on the NikeID website. However, only 24 pairs were made available per day until January 31, 2009. Fans who were able to customize their own pair of Kobe 4s had plenty of options. A full-team color palette, reptile design, and options for the leather.[95]

As Bryant cranked out points, Nike matched the output with marketing of the world's best basketball player. The commercials for the Kobe 4 portrayed an insurance company—specifically an ankle insurance company.[96] In the first ad, a disclaimer proclaims the following is a paid advertisement. Cut to Bryant, who introduces himself while dressed in a suit, sitting atop a horse.

The caption below him reads:

KOBE BRYANT
PRESIDENT and CEO and CFO and CMO and
OWNER y JEFE
ANKLE Insurance, Co.

Amateur players compete on the blacktop behind him. In a dramatic enactment, one of the players is crossed over and hits the ground in pain. Bryant continues to express the seriousness of ankle injuries and need for ankle insurance. In the following scene, he is in a testing facility clad in a black jumpsuit with the Kobe 4s on his feet. Bryant crosses over a test mannequin whose ankles explode into dust.

The commercial continues with testimonials from a team manager, a former player, a boy in a bubble, and a baby. Throughout the commercial, the narrator shouts, "Broken ankles!" to punctuate each scene. Following the testimonials, the narrator shouts that players will either buy the shoes and break ankles or have it done to them. On the screen, four boxes. On the left side of the screen, three boxes stacked with graphics of the Kobe 4 rotating. Each box is individually captioned: "SO LOW," "SO LIGHT," and "SO QUICK." The right half of the screen is dedicated to pictures of Bryant holding and admiring the revolutionary new sneaker.

Finally, Bryant is in an office, wearing a dress suit with the Kobe 4s on feet. In his best Don Draper impression, he makes his closing pitch on the importance of ankle insurance. He implores the audience to go to "NotMyBrokenAnkles.com." Mocking cheap and dramatic paid programming, the Kobe 4 commercial ventures well into absurdity. But it showed off Bryant's acting and comedic skills, which explain the enduring popularity of the nearly two-minute-long advertisement. Bryant's ankles would be safe in the Kobe 4.

Commercials weren't the only way Nike and Bryant were telling stories. With the Kobe 4, Nike released more colorways than ever. Many of them had special meanings to Bryant himself. From the winter of 2008 to fall 2009, Nike broke the mold of team colorways by introducing more energetic and captive colorways. The "Lower Merion Aces" and "MPLS" colorways had been around since the Kobe 1, and the "Carpe Diem" was used in the Kobe 2. All of which appeared again the Kobe 4 (and many more Kobe models to come).

The Kobe 4 gave us the "Chaos Joker" based on Bryant's love for Heath Ledger's performance in *The Dark Knight*. The sneaker used metallic silver and abyss-nightside colors to capture the Batman theme. The "Draft Day" was in Hornets colors since Charlotte had been the team to draft him. The date on the heel read "6.26.96" or, in some cases, "6.11.96." June 26, 1996 was the date of the 1996 NBA Draft.[97] Nobody is quite sure where the June 11, 1996 date came from and why it ended up on so many general release sneakers. But the error would stick with the colorway for years to come.

Nike continued taking a victory lap from the 2008 Olympics, so they released the Kobe 4 in the "Gold Medal" colorway. Despite wearing the Hyperdunks while playing in Beijing, the Kobe 4 used gold leather with a navy Swoosh across the side panels. The number 10 appeared on the heel instead of the usual 24. In a game against the Cavaliers on MLK Day, Bryant wore a pair of Kobe 4s in a tasteful colorway that featured a white and purple upper. The gold Swoosh, laces, and tongue are what set off the first "MLK" colorway in his line.

Other colorways such as the "Inline," "Del Sol," "Playoffs," and "Rice" were also introduced during Bryant's historic run in 2009.[98] After another hot start to the season, Bryant would be lacing up another pair of Kobe 4s in the "All Star" colorway that year in Phoenix—a straight-forward red-and-white colorway to match the Western Conference uniforms.

Bryant led the Western Conference in votes for the 2009 NBA All-Star Game. However, Dwight Howard of the Magic garnered over 3 million votes to lead the league and started for the Eastern Conference. After scoring 27 points, Bryant picked up his third NBA All-Star Game Most Valuable Player Award, only this time sharing it with Shaquille O'Neal. The former Laker had been traded from the Heat to the Suns and scored 17 points in less than 11 minutes of play.

It was a beautiful moment for the league. Bryant and O'Neal seemed to be reconciling. And the big man got the sendoff he deserved in his final NBA All-Star Game appearance. But the Black Mamba never was one for feel-good stories. He was still on a mission to win his fourth championship. Bryant led the Lakers to a 65-17 regular season record, which made them the 1-seed in the Western Conference Playoffs. Again, Bryant started in all 82 games, averaging 26.8 points, 4.9 assists, 5.2 rebounds, and 1.5 steals per game. Those ridiculous numbers put him on the All-NBA First Team and NBA All-Defensive First Team. However, the 2009 NBA Most Valuable Player Award went to LeBron James, who put together an equally stunning season.

Speaking of James, Nike was at it again with more commercials. During the spring of 2009, Nike debuted the first in a long series of commercials known as "Nike MVPuppets." The commercials featured Bryant and James puppets as roommates. In most of the commercials, the Kobe puppet played a self-centered caricature of his likeness. In contrast, the LeBron puppet did his best to remain calm and be respectful towards his elder. The commercials included gags about rings, throwing chalk in the air, jumping over cars, and throwing parties.[99] Timing for the commercials was perfect, given the MVP debates and the deep divide between Kobe and LeBron fans.

Before the end of the regular season, Bryant surprised school children in Chicago. He was the After-School All-Stars national ambassador, and Nike had teamed up with local elementary schools to organize a design competition.[100] The kids worked in groups on the NikeiD website to customize a pair of Kobe 4s, which Bryant would wear on the court against the Bulls.[101] The runner ups got a free pair of shoes from Nike. But the winning team witnessed in-person the perennial All-Star score 28 points while wearing the sneaker they designed.

Not long after the 2009 NBA Playoffs began, Spike Lee's documentary *Kobe Doin' Work* premiered on ESPN. The game the documentary focused on was the Spurs matchup from April 13, 2008. But Bryant's narration was recorded on February 2, 2009, after he cooked the Knicks in Madison Square Garden for 61 points. Throughout the documentary, Bryant gave fans insight on his strategy and thoughts during the game.

Some of the best moments from *Kobe Doin' Work* happened when Bryant wasn't on the court. Near the end of the documentary, Bryant greets his wife and two young daughters outside of the locker room. He discusses how he recently got them into Michael Jackson's *Thriller* as his oldest daughter, Natalia, does the dance from the music video. The family hops into a white Range Rover and drives off into the California sunset.

It was a picture-perfect scene for an incredible time in Bryant's career. The Lakers worked their way through a treacherous Western Conference playoff bracket. They defeated the Jazz in a 4-1 series, the Rockets in a 4-3 series, and finally the Nuggets in a 4-2 series. Following Game 6 of the 2009 Western Conference Finals, Bryant received a phone call from the hottest rapper in the world—Lil Wayne.

Bryant recounted the story in a 2018 episode of the Barstool Sports Podcast *The Corp With A-Rod and Big-Cat*. Apparently, Lil Wayne called Bryant and explained how his performance inspired him and asked Bryant if he could write a song. Bryant said, "I was like, all right, cool. I just thought he was BS-ing or whatever." But much to his surprise, Lil Wayne actually followed through on the song, which Bryant called "awesome."[102] The song titled "Kobe Bryant" served as the anthem for Lakers fans ever since its release. The chart-topper rapping about the All-Star further solidified Bryant's undeniable popularity.

After ripping through the Western Conference, Bryant led his team back to the NBA Finals. This time they would face the Magic and their NBA Defensive Player of the Year center Dwight Howard. Bryant wore Kobe 4 PEs specially designed for the NBA Finals. The home pair was white and purple, while the road pair was black and purple. Both PEs had his accolades printed across the upper.

Awards like All-Star and MVP were visible. Additionally, statistics such as points, assists, and minutes per game were also scrawled across the upper. After the Lakers defeated the Magic in a 4-1 series (which was closer than the number of games indicated), the Kobe 4 Finals PEs were available to fans. Albeit, the road colorway or "Finals MVP" had "MVP" on the tongue rather than the Kobe logo, which was what Bryant wore on the court.[103] The fourth championship for Bryant was tremendously important. The NBA Finals Most Valuable

Player proved to the world that he could win without O'Neal. And of course, he was one step closer to tying Lakers legend Magic Johnson's five championships.

Three days after clinching the franchise's 15th title, a championship parade was held in Downtown Los Angeles, which led to a rally held in the Los Angeles Memorial Coliseum. Bryant wore a Nike shirt, which featured a puppet's hand with and a ring on each of its four fingers.

On his feet, a pair of Kobe 4s in the "Del Sol—POP" or "Playoffs" colorway, the same sneaker he wore when he appeared as a guest on NBC's *The Tonight Show*. At the end of the interview, Bryant gave a pair to the new host of the show, Conan O'Brien, as a welcoming gift as he had recently moved to Los Angeles.[104]

Now would there finally be time for Bryant to rest? Of course not. In July, Bryant set off for the 2009 Nike Asia Tour. He hosted basketball clinics and other promotional events in six major cities: Manilla on July 21, Singapore on July 22, Taipei on July 23, Hong Kong on July 24, Shanghai on July 25, and Cheng Du on July 26.[105] Not only were Asian fans excited to see the reigning NBA Champion, but there was a new sneaker from the Kobe line to celebrate. The Nike Dream Season was a sneaker exclusive to Asia. There was no Flywire; it was a higher cut, and featured a more rugged outsole for playing outdoors.[106]

The Nike Dream Season would be the first of many different Kobe sneakers apart from his signature line. Nike began producing more budget-friendly sneakers that remained true to Bryant's vision of basketball footwear. Over the next decade, several different models were introduced: Kobe Venomenon, KB Mentality, Mamba Instinct, Mamba Rage, Mamba Focus, and the Mamba Fury. These sneakers would experiment with different ideas while keeping a low price point for consumers.

Not long after the summer celebrations ended and the confetti stopped flying in the air, it was time for the Lakers to defend their championship. During the offseason, Trevor Ariza left the team as a free agent, and the front office replaced him with Ron Artest. The bruising baller had battled the Lakers for years and quickly proved to be a major addition to the team that was more finesse and flash than grit and toughness.

Bryant, the new face of the NBA 2K10 video game, started the 2009-2010 season with a bang. On Opening Night, the Lakers defeated the Clippers 99-92 thanks to Bryant's 33 points and eight rebounds. On his feet that night, and for the first few months of the regular season, were Kobe 4 PEs. This time, Nike played with gradient colorways. Each colorway featured two colors that faded from one color to the next from the heel to the toe. Not only would Bryant wear these himself, but they were made available to the public.

The "Gradient Home" colorway started with a forum blue heel and tongue before transitioning into a white toe with a white Swoosh logo. On the flip side, the "Gradient Away" started with a forum blue heel and tongue before transitioning into a black toe with a gold Swoosh logo.[107] The home and away colorways were popular, but the "4 Rings" colorway took the cake. A gold heel and tongue transitioned into a dark purple toe and Swoosh. The insoles featured championship rings graphics to remind everyone of the monumental accomplishment that took place a few months earlier.[108]

Kobe V

Fans didn't want the stream of Kobe 4 colorways to end. That was, until Bryant debuted the Nike Zoom Kobe V on Christmas Day 2009 against the Cleveland Cavaliers. It would be a matchup of the previous two NBA Most Valuable Player Award winners: Kob' versus 'Bron. Even the MVPuppets had to get in on the action. Nike released Christmas themed commercials where Blitzen the Reindeer (voiced by Lupe Fiasco) and Santa (voiced by KRS-ONE) rapped about basketball and the holidays. In the third installment, Bryant and James played against the reindeer, and assured viewers that no reindeer were harmed despite the puppets dunking on their furry animal friends.

The Cavaliers easily won 102-87 that day. But the Kobe 5 made a strong first impression thanks to Bryant's 35 points in the "Joker" colorway. Designer Eric Avar followed Bryant's request to shave more weight and materials off the sneaker. The Kobe 5 utilized a full synthetic "Skinwire" upper, except for mesh used around a noticeably lower heel collar. The external TPU heel counter is significantly slimmed down compared to its predecessor and has Bryant's signature printed rather than the number 24.

For more breathability, Nike utilized its Torch technology on the bottom three-fourths of the tongue (the top of the tongue had a synthetic coating with the Kobe logo). Perforations were made on the toe cap and lateral side of the sneaker to aid in keeping the foot from sweating too much. No major changes were made with cushion. The design team kept the phylon midsole with a large Zoom Air unit in the heel and a small Zoom Air unit under the ball of the foot.[109] As always, there was ample padding on the interior of the sneaker for more comfort.

A rubber outsole took the design of an EKG pattern. It was all one color except for the Kobe logo located on the heel, and a rectangular block of contrasting color highlighted the pivot point. A thin piece of carbon fiber in the middle of the outsole and a lateral outrigger added support for the incredibly narrow sneaker. The Kobe 5 continued to design a basketball sneaker that mimicked a soccer cleat—only weighing 10.6 ounces (men's size 9) while still providing adequate support.[110]

This time around NikeiD was more widely available. Earlier in the month, Nike hosted a special media event at the Montalban Theatre in Los Angeles to introduce the Kobe 5 and the different customization options. Colors, materials, and graphics were all up to the consumer now. There were individual computers set up for attendees to put their twist on the new sneaker at the event. Three important dates for the NikeiD process appeared on a large screen. Beginning on December 10, fans were able to build and share their designs online. However, they wouldn't be able to purchase them until December 25.[111] Additionally, more colors and graphics became available in 2010.

Fans, hoopers, sneakerheads, and Kobe-fanatics alike spent countless hours in front of their computer screen, fulfilling their dream of customizing his newest signature shoe. There is no telling how much productivity was lost at school and work with this new option available to basketball fans. The NikeiD options for the Kobe 5 were nice, but the general release colorways of the sneaker were even better. The "Draft Day," "MLK," "Carpe Diem," "Lower Merion Aces," "Dark Knight," "Inline," "Rice," and of course, the "Home" and "Away" colorways were all back.[112]

Another All-Star Game colorway released after Bryant got the second-most votes in the league (behind only LeBron James). Bryant would miss the 2010 NBA All-Star Game due to injury, but it wouldn't stop Nike from releasing a pair of red-and-black Kobe 5s to mark the event. It was hard to believe, but Nike dropped more heat for fans. "Duke" and "USC" colorways were dropped in their respective school colors before March Madness. But there are few recurring colorways in the Kobe line that are more important than the "Bruce Lee" introduced in February of 2010. The gold-and-black colorway had four red claw marks near the laces to pay homage to the martial arts icon.

The colors fit Lakers uniforms, but what they were actually doing was paying homage to the jumpsuit worn by Lee in the 1978 movie *The Game of Death*. Nike released several promotional posters of Bryant striking the same poses as Lee in his most popular films.[113] The commercial for the Kobe 5 brought back the MVPuppet for one of his final appearances. The Kobe puppet freestyled with two puppets dressed as Foot Locker employees behind him, echoing his bars. An "Away" colorway in his hand got so hot it caught fire, which required Lil Dez (a sidekick from previous commercials) to extinguish the flames.

While Nike took care of the marketing, Bryant took care of the competition on the court. The Lakers finished the regular season with a record of 57-25, which was good enough to be the 1-seed in the Western Conference. LeBron James, not Kobe Bryant, would win the 2010 NBA Most Valuable Player Award. However, Bryant did get named to All-NBA First Team and NBA All-Defensive First Team yet again. Bryant started in all 73 games he played while leading the team with 27 points, five assists, and 1.6 steals in 38.8 minutes per game.

In the first round of the playoffs, an upstart Thunder team consisting of Kevin Durant, Russell Westbrook, and James Harden challenged the Lakers before eventually losing the series 4-2. The next round was a breeze as the Lakers swept the Jazz 4-0. Finally, in the Western Conference Finals, the Lakers eliminated the Steve Nash-led Suns 4-2 in the final meeting between the two teams in the playoffs.

One final hurdle stood in the way between Bryant and the history books. The Celtics were back in the NBA Finals after marching through the Eastern Conference bracket. Boston's Big 3 had eliminated Dwyane Wade and the Heat in a 4-1 series. They embarrassed LeBron James and the Cavaliers in a 4-2 series. Lastly, in the Eastern Conference Finals, they outplayed Dwight Howard and the Magic in a 4-2 series.

It was clear the Lakers had to play tougher and more physical than ever if they wanted to avoid the same results as the 2008 NBA Finals. Bryant went into the series with several nagging injuries and needed to rely on his footwear to support him.

Nike capitalized on Bryant's NBA Finals appearance by putting together another classic commercial that appealed to fans of all age groups and backgrounds. Hip-hop artist Andre 3000 put his Southern twist on the Beatles song "All Together Now." The song synced up perfectly with highlights. The commercial began with the song's opening notes while showing Bryant's buzzer-beater against the Heat from earlier in the season. As Andre 3000 began singing, a replay showed Bryant celebrating his fourth championship the year before.

As the song and tempo progressed, clips of Bryant alongside other NBA legends continued to play. Past characters in Nike commercials, Lil' Penny and Mars Blackmon, appear in the commercial with impressed looks on their faces. The final lyrics kept repeating and speeding up each time. The clips whip viewers into a frenzy. MVPuppet Lil Dez had to hit his inhaler. Finally, the song hits its crescendo and slows down for the final scene, a cheering crowd and a softly smiling Bryant giving the nod. The commercial ends with a grainy screen that reads "just do it" before switching to the Swoosh logo and "facebook.com/nikebasketball" in the bottom right corner of the screen.[114]

Throughout the seven-game slugfest, Bryant wore the Kobe 5 "Big Stage" in home and away colorways. The "Big Stage Away" colorway was all black with a gold Swoosh, heel, and Kobe logo, while the "Big Stage Home" colorway was all white with a gold Swoosh, heel, and Kobe logo. Both sneakers featured Bryant's achievements from the season in tattoo-style graphics.[115]

On the lateral side, "25,970" was his total career points by the end of the regular season, "73" represented how many regular-season games he played, and a star logo signified his All-Star selection. On the sneaker's medial side, you see "2,835" for the total minutes played, "113" for total steals, "365" for total assists, "391" for total rebounds, "27" for average points per game that season.

On the toe cap, "02.01.10" with "All-Time" just below it, reminding everyone of the day he passed Kareem Abdul-Jabbar for most points in a Lakers uniform. A black mamba snakeskin was printed on the upper and intertwined with the accolades to enhance the tattoo-style graphics. Both colorways were a part of a limited release later that summer on August 6 in select retailers and at www.kb24.com.[116]

Game 7 of the series was low-scoring and ultra-physical. Bryant scored 23 points and grabbed 15 rebounds. Pau Gasol totaled 19 points and 18 rebounds. Ron Artest tallied 20 points, including a game-sealing three-pointer. The Lakers would emerge victorious 83-79. One of the enduring images from the game is Bryant grabbing the ball as time expired and looking back towards his teammates with absolute glee on his face. On his feet are the Kobe 5 "Big Stage Home" colorway.

Bryant had done it. Not only had he won his fifth championship (tying Magic Johnson), but he'd earned his second NBA Finals Most Valuable Player Award. All of his determination and belief in himself paid off. He weathered the storms. His success and popularity outlasted and surpassed his contemporaries. He was Nike's golden goose. He was the biggest name in the entertainment capital of the world. He would be shaking hands with President Barack Obama for a second straight year.

At long last, Kobe Bryant was king of the basketball world.

CHAPTER 7

Lows

Fresh off consecutive championships, Bryant took a working vacation to South Africa for the 2010 FIFA World Cup. He attended the second-round match where Ghana eliminated the United States 2-1. Although Nike wasn't an official event sponsor, they did have a presence at the festivities. Bryant showed up to a state-of-the-art practice facility in Soweto, where he surprised campers.[117] Draped in a black jumpsuit with a pair of Kobe 5s in the "Del Sol" colorway on his feet, Bryant displayed his fluency in foreign languages and soccer knowledge.

There would soon be a lot more travel for Bryant. His quest for a sixth championship and another Lakers three-peat would start with the 2010 NBA Europe Live Tour. The two-time defending champions played preseason exhibition games in London and Barcelona, complete with media events in both cities.[118] Bryant wore the same pair of Kobe 5 PEs in a simple white-and-gold colorway throughout the entire tour. In an inauspicious start to the 2010-2011 season, the Lakers lost to the Timberwolves in London and Regal FC Barcelona of the Euroleague in Barcelona. The Lakers were unfazed by the losses, and maybe they were right not to be concerned.

The regular season began with the Lakers rattling off eight straight wins before cooling off in November and December. Bryant wore Kobe 5 PEs until an all-important Christmas Day matchup against the Heat in Los Angeles. A new "Big 3" in the Eastern Conference formed when LeBron James took his talents to South Beach to team up with Chris Bosh and Dwyane Wade.

Kobe VI

In an embarrassing 96-80 loss to the Heat, Bryant debuted what many people consider to be his most popular sneaker of all time, the Nike Zoom Kobe VI "Grinch." The colorway featured a lime green upper, black Swoosh, and red laces to match the Kobe logo. It was no secret that Bryant enjoyed stealing happiness away from his opponents, which made him the perfect candidate for a colorway to match the dubious Dr. Seuss character.

The colorway and storytelling were perfect, but the sneaker itself continued to push the envelope of performance footwear. Designer Eric Avar created a sneaker that screamed Black Mamba. The upper consisted of three layers: Flywire, a thin layer of mesh, and most noticeably polyurethane on top that looked and felt like snakeskin. The plastic texture was for more than just appearance; it provided protection and support for the foot.

Thanks to perforations throughout the scaly upper, the sneaker was more ventilated than its predecessors. Nike used its Torch system on the tongue's inner sleeve again to make for a cool ride. Lockdown for the low-profile model was provided by the carved-out external TPU heel counter. The hard rubber outsole featured an aggressive snakeskin traction pattern with three prominent flex grooves carved out in the forefoot for a natural stepping motion.[119] A Kobe logo sat under the narrow heel of the outsole connected to a wider forefoot by a carbon fiber plate in the midfoot. The cushion consisted of a phylon midsole with a large-volume Nike Zoom Air unit under the heel and a smaller unit under the ball of the foot. A dual-density foam sockliner coupled with a thick insole added more comfort for long stints on the hardwood.

Branding was all over the Kobe 6. A large Swoosh sat on both the medial and lateral sides of the sneaker, with the Kobe logo on the tongue, the word "Venomenon" on the toe, and the continuation of "Kobe Code" on the lateral outrigger (a dot-matrix language sequence that first appeared on the Kobe 5). Not only did the aesthetics of the Kobe 6 match Bryant's persona, but it was a technological triumph. The sneaker weighed just 10.6 ounces (men's size 9) without sacrificing the safety of players. General release colorways would cost sneakerheads $130 for the best technology available at the time.

In a Nike press release on December 7, Bryant's quote read, "The Kobe VI is a very character-driven shoe with the alter ego of the Black Mamba prominently featured. We continue to evolve the technology to make it a performance-based shoe, but aesthetically you haven't seen a shoe pop like this before. It brings to life what drives me."[120]

Compared to designing the newest model, the marketing would be the easy part. NikeiD gave a sneak preview to Facebook fans on December 10, while the public would be able to purchase their customized sneakers two weeks later on Christmas Eve.[121] Consumers would have more customization options than ever before. They were able to play with wild new color palettes and even modify the outsoles for $165.

Family friend and *SLAM* Magazine Contributor Anthony Gilbert was fascinated by the change in direction of Kobe's signature sneaker line. Gilbert said, "As the tide changed with the release of the IV, V, and VI— those shoes were a game-changer for him and Nike. He was always looking for an advantage on the court, so he wanted the low-cut shoe to allow his ankle and foot to move more freely. He won his fourth championship in the Kobe IV against the Orlando Magic, his fifth ring in the Kobe V against the Celtics. I saw it as poetic to match his signature shoe with his championship accomplishments."[122]

The commercial for the Kobe 6 continued to use humor to poke fun at Bryant's ultra-competitive instincts. The ad starts with a Foot Locker employee lacing up the new sneaker on a customer and assuring him that the new Kobes would make him a beast. With a determined look on his face and a pair of Kobe 6s in the "Concord" colorway on his feet, the customer takes off running out of the store. Never missing a beat, he runs through several different settings while continuously making spectacular plays. The man runs through pickup and organized games alike, people's homes, and arcades. He even dominates a boxing match and a game of bingo. Finally, he returns to the store to say he'll buy the sneakers after all.[123]

Following the Christmas Day game, Bryant took the court in a series of Kobe 6 PEs for the remainder of the season. Thanks to another tremendous start to the season, Bryant led the league in All-Star votes. To make matters even better, Bryant won the 2011 NBA All-Star Game Most Valuable Player Award in front of his home fans in Staples Center. It would mark the fourth and final time he would win the award.

Bryant used the opportunity to debut the Kobe 6 "All-Star" in a red-and-black colorway. That sneaker and three other pairs would be made available to the public in limited quantities as part of the "Nike Kobe 6 All-Star Pack." Over the course of a month, Nike released the "East LA" in a nearly all-blue colorway. The "Hollywood/3D" colorway using gray, red, and blue to create a three-dimensional appearance. Lastly, the "Orange County/Sunset," a colorway that transitioned from a bright orange toe to a black heel.

Keeping with tradition, Nike brought back many fan-favorite colorways. "Chaos," "Dark Knight," "Del Sol," "Draft Day," "Lower Merion," and "BHM" (Black History Month would be used instead of "MLK"), were all reintroduced through the Kobe 6. Meanwhile, new stories were being told through colorways. Several different "Camo" and "Gradient" colorways, two "Barcelona" colorways as part of a pack, and an all-pink "Think Pink" colorway were all made available to the public.[124]

Unfortunately, the Kobe 6 was the last appearance of the "Rice" colorway. Rice High School in Harlem had become well-known for its outstanding basketball talent and equally successful academic programs. Due to the economic realities of the time, the school closed down in the spring of 2011. The Nike-sponsored school had been adopted by Bryant several years earlier, and always received the latest Kobe PEs to match their green-and-gold school colors. The Hyperdunks and Kobes 1-6 all got the Rice treatment and have become some of the more coveted sneakers in the vast Kobe sneaker line.[125]

Jarrel Harris, NBA and Sneakers editor for *Sports Illustrated*, graduated from Rice High School. Although Harris played baseball, not basketball, he was still impacted by Nike and Bryant. Harris says, "Kobe's presence had a major impact on the entire school. Rice had a strong relationship with Nike, and that is how the Kobe connection was made. LeBron James has a similar relationship with Christ the King located in Queens. Kobe usually made trips to Harlem to visit our school when the Lakers were in town to play the Knicks or Nets and hung out with the team."

Harris recalls, "I remember it was on Super Bowl Sunday in 2009 when Nike and Kobe invited the basketball team to Foot Locker to showcase the Zoom Kobe IV and unveiled a special PE for the upcoming CHSAA Championship game. Through the relationship with Kobe, Rice was able to wear and release many legendary Kobe PEs that we still see on NBA courts today. It is kind of surreal to see that my school, which shut down in 2011, is still represented in some form on the court."[126]

By this time, Bryant's teammates started wanting in on the heat. Lakers Equipment Manager Rudy Garciduenas recalls, "A good portion of his teammates who did not have their own shoe deals wanted to be in his shoes. When he came out with the lower models, they were not so receptive to them. The consensus in the league still was that a higher shoe was needed for ankle protection. In the later years, when he became more creative with graphics on the shoes, his teammates really like those."[127]

The only thing more stunning than the sheer volume of Kobe 6s released was the output from their namesake. Again, Bryant started in all 82 games of the regular season, averaging 25.3 points, 4.7 assists, and 1.2 steals per game. Those numbers put him on the All-NBA First Team as well as NBA All-Defensive First Team. Thanks to another vintage season from the Black Mamba, the Lakers went 57-25, which earned them the 2-seed in the Western Conference Playoffs. After defeating the Hornets in a 4-2 series, the two-time defending champions would get swept out of the playoffs by the Mavericks. The run was finally over. Another three-peat for Bryant and Jackson was not in the cards.

There is no doubt the physical stress of the past three seasons played a role in the Lakers coming up short. But that is dismissive of how good the Mavericks were that season. Led by Dirk Nowitzki, Dallas won the 2011 NBA Finals over Miami's "Big 3" in a 4-2 series. After an early playoff exit, Coach Phil Jackson retired from the Lakers for the final time. By late May, the front office had agreed to a four-year deal with Mike Brown to take over as the 22nd coach in franchise history.

After serving as the Lakers Equipment Manager for 26 years, Rudy Garciduenas was also one of the many staff changes made during the summer of 2011. Garciduenas reflected on his time by saying, "I took care of many players during my tenure with the Lakers, but Kobe was definitely special. We didn't always see eye to eye because I constantly had to remind him of the league's guidelines and restrictions, but we managed. I will always treasure those experiences."[128]

Over the offseason, Bryant worked on recovering from injuries and continuing his marketing efforts with Nike. In July, he kicked off another Asian tour that further solidified his rockstar status on the continent. Bryant took part in various events, in multiple countries.[129]

Due to a labor dispute, Bryant had to wait out the second work stoppage of his career. Unverified rumors flew around from all different angles about Bryant potentially signing a short-term contract with various teams in different foreign leagues. However, he did surprise fans by playing in an exhibition game at the Drew League.

The Drew League is a pro-am (professional-amateur) basketball league held in Los Angeles every summer. During the 2011 NBA Lockout, several notable players made the pilgrimage to play in the historic league. But none of them were more popular and more meaningful to fans than Bryant. After being snuck in through a special entrance and dressing in his own locker room, Bryant walked onto the court as fans erupted.[130]

In front of an overflow crowd, Bryant dropped 43 points, including a game-winner against a team led by Thunder star James Harden. The perennial All-NBA player wore a purple uniform with the number 20 on the back and a pair of Kobe 6s in a white-and-gray colorway. It was the only time Bryant played in the Drew League. However, it would be far from the last time he made sneaker news at the event.

After a 149-day lockout, the 2011-2012 season was set to begin on Christmas Day. There would be 66 regular season games built on a grueling travel schedule. Just before the season, there appeared to be big news for the Lakers. On December 8, a trade was reported that would have sent Chris Paul to the Lakers, Paul Gasol to the Rockets, and Lamar Odom (along with several Houston players and a draft pick) to the Hornets.

Within a few hours, news broke that the trade would not go through. NBA spokesman Tim Frank said the "league office declined to make the trade for basketball reasons."[131] At the time, the league managed the Hornets franchise. Several other team owners complained about the fairness of the trade, so the deal was off. A few days later, Chris Paul was traded to Los Angeles to play for the Clippers. Lakers fans and players were upset about the trade for years to come.

Kobe VII

One thing that pleased everyone was the early release of the Nike Kobe VII System Supreme. Once again, Nike reimagined what was possible in a performance basketball sneaker, and the Kobe line was their canvas. The major change in the Kobe 7 was the introduction of the "Kobe System Supreme." Two different midsoles came with the sneaker to fit different play styles.[132] The "Attack Fast" option featured a phylon midsole with Nike Zoom Air units in the heel and forefoot. A low-cut insert with a breathable cuff that hugged the midfoot. The "Attack Fast" option lent itself to players with a game predicated on quickness and agility.

The second option, the "Attack Strong" midsole, was full-length Cushlon with a padded sensory cuff that supported the ankle. The goal of the ankle cuff was to promote tactile stimulation (awareness on the foot's location). The "Attack Strong" option was geared towards more powerful players.

The Kobe 7s upper consisted of next-generation Flywire with a cast polyurethane outer shell and a sizable Swoosh on both sides. A 3D heel counter sporting Bryant's signature aided in keeping the foot secure. Nike mixed the best of both worlds on its hard rubber outsole. A triangular traction spanned from the heel to the lateral outrigger, while a herringbone traction pattern covered the pivot point and ball of the foot. For added support and torsional rigidity, Nike used a glass-reinforced carbon shank plate.

Performance versatility was one of the key elements of the "Kobe System." The customization didn't stop at the tooling. The Kobe 7s upper "skin" featured a design consisting of three predators—the leopard, the great white shark, and the black mamba. A separate graphic pattern was under the skin of some colorways—a leopard, great white shark, poison dart frog, and gray wolf.[133] Different animal, same beast. At a Nike event in December of 2011, Bryant told the story of how the safari trip he'd taken while in South Africa inspired him. He was more interested in the predators than the prey. That's when it hit him—he wanted a line that embodied his predatory style on the court.

The Nike Kobe 7 System Supreme with the two interchangeable midsoles cost $180. In comparison, the Kobe 7 System, which only included the low-cut "Attack Fast" midsole, was $140. As always, NikeiD tantalized fans by offering a sneak peek December 12 on Facebook. On December 22, the public would be able to purchase their customized Kobe 7s. Nike continued to expand the plethora of options they offered for customization.

Beginning December 22, three of Nike's marquee basketball sneakers would go virtual in the video game NBA2K12. The Kobe 7 "Cheetah" colorway alongside a pair of LeBron 9s and KD 4s were part of a Christmas Pack available to gamers. Throughout the year, specific colorways launched in the game at key moments.[134] The Nike Kobe line remained in every iteration of NBA2K from that point forward.

Nike enlisted some of the biggest names in the world to film a series of commercials known as the "Kobe System: Success for the Successful" campaign: Richard Branson, Aziz Ansari, Tony Robbins, Serena Williams, Hope Solo, LeeHom Wang, Larry Fitzgerald, Jerry Rice, Landon Donovan, Paul Rodriguez, and of course, Kanye West.[135]

In the ad campaign, Bryant took on the role of a motivational speaker. The titans of their respective industries sat in the crowd and quizzed Bryant with questions on finding even more success. Bryant responded with empty answers that implied they do more. In the commercial titled "Level 6 Beastion," Bryant challenged and confused West.

> *West*: How much more do you want from me?
> *Bryant*: More.
> *West*: How much more successful do you want me

to be?
Bryant: *More successful.*
West: *How many records can my records break?*
Bryant: *More records.*
West: *But . . . I'm the best.*
Bryant: *But are you a different animal and the same beast?*
West: *What the [bleep] does that mean, Kobe Bryant?*
Bryant: *You're welcome.*
West: *What the [bleep] is he talking about?*

The commercial ended with the message: "ATTACK FAST. ATTACK STRONG. LEARN THE SYSTEM @NIKEBASKETBALL." Triangular designs were prominent in the marketing of the Kobe 7 System. Everyone in the commercial had a triangle pin on their lapel. Triangles were on the screens behind Bryant. Pictures of Bryant and the other celebrities holding up a triangle hand gesture were all over the internet. Hence why the outsole of the Kobe 7 featured a triangular traction pattern.

After a longer than usual offseason for Bryant, the Lakers season tipped off on Christmas Day. As time ran out in the game, Bryant took the ball to the rim against three Bulls defenders but couldn't get the basket or a foul call. The Bulls took the game 88-87. Despite the rough start to the season, Bryant continued to pass NBA legends in the record books. The 32-year-old had played a lot of minutes in the league, and the cumulation of career achievements were adding up quickly. Another career year meant another All-Star appearance. Bryant led the Western Conference in votes, but he was second in the league to Dwight Howard who was playing in front of his home crowd in Orlando, Florida.

The 2012 NBA All-Star Game was memorable for several reasons. Dwyane Wade broke Bryant's nose (which resulted in "Masked Mamba" the next few weeks). Bryant poured in 27 points in a Western Conference win. Also, Bryant debuted a pair of Kobe 7 Systems in the "Galaxy" colorway. The "Attack Fast" version of the sneaker featured a supernova-print upper with metallic silver Swooshes and a glow-in-the-dark outsole.

Due to the Kobe 7 System being such a departure from previous models, there were not many of the familiar colorways. A "Barcelona" pack, "BHM," "Black Del Sol," "Concord," "Duke," and "Lower Merion Aces" all made a return, while many new colorways made an appearance—multiple "Poison Dart Frog" colorways, "Cheetah," "Shark," "Snow Leopard," "Wolf Grey," "Year of the Dragon," and "Yin and Yang."[136]

An important new colorway Nike introduced in all of their signature athletes' basketball lines was the "What The" colorways. A mash-up of several different colorways and themes resulting in a loud sneaker that fans either loved or hated. The only thing more eye-catching than what Bryant had on his feet was what he was doing with the ball in the last half of 2012. The Lakers finished 41-25 in the regular season and earned the 3-seed in the Western Conference playoffs. Bryant started in 58 games while leading the team with averages of 27.9 points and 1.2 steals per game in 38.5 minutes. The media voted Bryant to All-NBA First Team again, but only an NBA All-Defensive Second Team for the first time since 2002.

In the first round of the playoffs, the Lakers squeaked past the Nuggets in a 4-3 series. The Western Conference Semifinals were even more challenging. The upstart Thunder had finally reached their full maturation and took care of the Lakers in a gentleman's sweep 4-1. It wasn't without Bryant going for 42 points in the final playoff game of his career. The torch had been passed. The Thunder would advance out of the Western Conference before losing to the Heat in the 2012 NBA Finals.

After another early playoff exit, Bryant resumed his grueling training and travel schedule. In August, he would team up with other NBA All-Stars to compete in the 2012 Summer Olympics held in London. Similar to his most recent experience in the playoffs, the torch had been passed on the United States Men's National Basketball Team as well. Kevin Durant and LeBron James led the team to another gold medal. But Bryant didn't travel all the way to London to not make some noise. He averaged 12.1 points, 1.8 rebounds, and 1.3 steals per game. On his feet was the Kobe 7 System, in a patriotic "USA" colorway, which released as part of a pack in limited quantities in late September.[137]

After securing his second gold medal, Bryant took off for another continent. From August 15-17, Bryant hosted his seventh China tour. As part of Nike's "Find Your Greatness" campaign, he made stops in Jinan, Wuhan, and Guangzhou. Bryant received love at every stop, including four thousand fans waiting for him in Jinan.[138] Bryant continued to wear the Kobe 7 System throughout the summer and fall. On September 27, the Lakers Instagram account posted a picture of orange Nike boxes stacked deep enough to build a fort. The caption read, "Equipment man Carlos Maples estimates that he's got 150 pairs of shoes waiting for Kobe. Here's some."[139]

Dr. Tim DiFrancesco was the Head Strength and Conditioning Coach for the Lakers from 2011-2017 and recalled the sheer volume of Nike gear that Maples had to manage. DiFrancesco said, "He [Maples] had an entire garage-size section of the equipment room that was dedicated to what equipment needed to be there for Kobe. And a lot of players wore his shoes and wanted some of his other gear from Nike. There was a lot they had to account for in ways other teams didn't have to."[140]

After traveling the globe during the summer, Bryant had new teammates to greet at training camp the following fall. Through a series of roster moves, the Lakers brought in Steve Nash and Dwight Howard. A *Sports Illustrated* cover declared, "Now This Is Going To Be Fun." In fact, the season was anything but fun. The Lakers went 0-8 in the preseason, then started the regular season 1-4. Coach Mike Brown was fired, and Bernie Bickerstaff took over as the interim head coach. Despite media speculation about Phil Jackson returning, the front office instead hired Mike D'Antoni. There was a sense of desperation about the team, and Bryant couldn't wait much longer to debut his newest sneaker.

Kobe 8

The Nike Kobe 8 System, designed by Eric Avar and his team in collaboration with Kobe Bryant, continued to reshape performance footwear. Nike used Engineered Mesh for the first time in a basketball sneaker. Meanwhile, 2013 was the Chinese Year of the Snake, which inspired the snakeskin design on the mesh upper. A 3D anatomical heel counter locked the foot into place on top of a full-length Lunarlon drop-in midsole. A one-millimeter outsole used a mix of herringbone and snakeskin traction patterns, while a carbon fiber plate added support for the incredibly flexible sneaker. Besides the snakeskin print on the upper, branding was all over the Kobe 8 System. A Swoosh on both sides of the foot, Kobe logo on the tongue and heel of the outsole, Kobe signature on the heel counter, and more mysterious "Kobe Code" imprinted on the outsole.

On NikeiD, fans were able to start their personal design process on December 4 and purchase them beginning on December 20. Fans would be able to choose from four midsole options. This excerpt describing the options is taken directly from the NIKE Press Release from November 29, 2012:[141]

> *"NIKEiD will offer various performance and style customization options for the KOBE 8 SYSTEM shoe, enabling consumers to create their own player edition. Consumers can choose from four midsole options: Lunarlon cushioning for a soft yet responsive ride, or an orthotic-ready Nike Zoom insert which is super-thin and sits lower to the ground than traditional midsole inserts. And for players who want to track and measure their game with Nike+ Basketball, there are two additional midsole options: the KOBE+ 8 SYSTEM SP+ (which comes bundled with the Nike+ Sport Kit) or the KOBE 8 SYSTEM EN+ midsole for players who previously purchased the Nike+ Sport Kit (sold separately)."*

The Kobe 8 System was lighter, lower, and more minimal than ever. At 9.6 ounces (men's size 9), it was the lightest sneaker in Kobe's signature line. General release colorways were available starting on December 20 for $140.[142]

Television advertisements for the Nike Kobe 8 System were much more toned down from the previous year. The "#CountOnKobe" commercial took a more humorous approach comparing Bryant to the natural phenomena of the world, while the second commercial only focused on the sneakers and their technology. Both advertisements heavily played up the obvious snake theme that existed in the Kobe 8 System.[143]

Not long after Bryant debuted the "Christmas" colorway against the Knicks, fans got another treat from the Black Mamba. On January 4, 2013, Bryant sent out his first tweet: "The antisocial has become social #mambatweets."[144] Social media was now another tool in Bryant's arsenal. He would often send out gnarly pictures of the injuries he sustained on the court.

The 2013 NBA All-Star Game took place in Houston. Bryant led the league in total votes and used the opportunity to bust out one of the flashiest colorways in the history of his signature line. Bryant wore a pair of Kobe 8 System+ in the "All Star—Extraterrestrial" colorway. A bright citrus-orange upper with a turquoise Swoosh and laces. The spacey theme was part of Nike Basketball's "Area 72" collection inspired by Houston's history with NASA. It marked the debut of Nike+ technology on the Kobe 8 System. Fans could get the Sport Pack for $280 and the regular Nike+ version for $195.[145]

General release colorways for the Kobe 8 System didn't disappoint. "Barcelona," "BHM," and "What The Kobe" were all brought back. Nike introduced the "Easter" and "Mambacurial" colorways, which were here to stay. Meanwhile, there were dozens of colorways based on different types of snakes, camo colorways, and the Chinese Zodiac.[146] Even Nike couldn't keep up with Bryant's output during the back half of the 2013 schedule. After an abysmal start to the season, followed by countless injuries, Bryant put the team on his back.

One of the most memorable games became known as the "Amnesty Game." Dallas Mavericks owner Mark Cuban suggested the Lakers front office should use the amnesty provision on Bryant. The amnesty provision, a part of the CBA, allowed teams to waive a player's contract without suffering a salary cap hit. The player still received their full salary but could not resign with the team that waived him. Bryant responded to the ridiculous suggestion on February 24, 2013, by torching the Mavericks for 38 points, 12 rebounds, and seven assists in a 103-99 Lakers win. Following the game, Bryant sub-tweeted at Cuban. His tweet read, "Amnesty THAT."[147]

The Lakers finished the season on a 25-11 streak to sneak into the playoffs. Sadly, the man who got them there wouldn't be able to compete in the playoffs, or months to come. Bryant started in 78 games while averaging 27.3 points, six assists, and 1.4 steals per game. The 34-year-old played 38.6 minutes per game before his body finally gave out on him. After scoring 32 points in a must-win game against the Warriors, Bryant made a move towards the basket and immediately hit the floor. He suffered a ruptured Achilles tendon. Teammates surrounded him as he pinched the tendon, trying to roll it back down into place. Bryant sauntered to the free throw line and sank both free throws before walking off the floor under his own power.

A despondent Bryant answered questions for the media following the game. Then around 3:30 a.m. PT, he went on a lengthy Facebook rant for the ages[148]:

> *This is such BS! All the training and sacrifice just flew out the window with one step that I've done millions of times! The frustration is unbearable. The anger is rage. Why the hell did this happen ?!? Makes no damn sense. Now I'm supposed to come back from this and be the same player Or better at 35?!? How in the world am I supposed to do that??*
> *I have NO CLUE. Do I have the consistent will to overcome this thing? Maybe I should break out the rocking chair and reminisce on the career that was. Maybe this is how my book ends. Maybe Father Time has defeated me . . . Then again maybe not! It's 3:30am, my foot feels like dead weight, my head is spinning from the pain meds and I'm wide awake. Forgive my Venting but what's the purpose of social media if I won't bring it to you Real No Image?? Feels good to vent, let it out. To feel as if THIS is the WORST thing EVER! Because After ALL the venting, a real perspective sets in. There are far greater issues/challenges in the world then a torn achilles. Stop feeling sorry for yourself, find the silver lining and get to work with the same belief, same drive and same conviction as ever.*
> *One day, the beginning of a new career journey will commence. Today is NOT that day.*
> *"If you see me in a fight with a bear, prey for the bear." Ive always loved that quote. Thats 'mamba mentality' we don't quit, we don't cower, we don't run. We endure and conquer.*
> *I know it's a long post but I'm Facebook Venting LOL. Maybe now I can actually get some sleep and be excited for surgery tomorrow. First step of a new*

challenge.
Guess I will be Coach Vino the rest of this season. I have faith in my teammates. They will come thru. Thank you for all your prayers and support. Much Love Always.
Mamba Out

Like other NBA veterans, Bryant was no stranger to the injuries that come with playing basketball, such as painful sprains and strains. But Bryant had already overcome a broken right wrist, an avulsion fracture in his right index finger, tenosynovitis in his right shin, a torn right labrum in his shoulder that required surgery, and multiple operations and procedures on his knees. But a ruptured Achilles tendon is different. Not only does it require a lengthy recovery time, but it's a career-threatening injury.

Bryant was named to All-NBA First Team for his gutsy performance that season. The Lakers would get swept in the first round of the playoffs by the Spurs. Adding insult to injury, Dwight Howard left during free agency that summer. Meanwhile, Bryant used his personal Instagram account to post every single hurdle he cleared on his road to recovery. Posts included a gory picture of his Achilles mid-operation and a candid video of him speaking with his surgeon months later. Bryant even had some fun with a meme of a walking boot with a crudely photoshopped Kobe logo and Nike Swoosh on the side. Beside the boot someone had put: "#KOBESYSTEM DOMINATE ACHILLES."[149]

All jokes aside, Nike didn't waste time in constructing the ideal shoe for Bryant's recovery. On May 30, Bryant posted a photo of himself walking on an anti-gravity treadmill. The caption read, "Walking in my 'medical mamba' shoes made by Nike in 2 weeks with extra support for the Achilles #alterG #bootoff!"[150]

CHAPTER 8

Highs

In mid-July, Bryant hosted the seventh-annual Kobe Bryant Basketball Academy at the University of California, Santa Barbara. Naturally, everyone's eyes were on the feet of the recently injured superstar. Bryant wore a pair of Kobe 8 PEs in the "Graffiti" colorway but in a mid-cut design.[151] The "Graffiti" colorway was released to the public the following month but kept the usual low-cut design for general release.

Lakers Head Strength and Conditioning Coach, Dr. Tim DiFrancesco, worked with Bryant throughout the recovery. He remembered the mid-cut but wasn't sure about the origin of the specially designed sneaker. In our phone interview, DiFrancesco said, "I don't know if that's something he requested. I know that he often had a lot input on what his shoes looked like, so I have to imagine some of that came from him. It gave him the ability to feel some extra support there and gave him a chance to get a new look on a previous model."[152]

Chris Chase of WearTesters.com was also unsure about the exact reasoning for the specially designed mid-cut but had his theories. In an email, he said, "The lower collar might have rested close to the rupture or incision location, thus making the mid more comfortable to wear. He and Nike could have also been wear-testing to see which collar height he'd feel was best for upcoming models such as the future Nike Kobe A.D. Mid—one of Kobe's post-retirement models. They really could have been made for any number of reasons."[153]

In early August, Bryant was met by tens of thousands of fans when he returned to China. One of those fans was a young man who goes by the alias of Xinjie. The nervous 19-year-old got to speak with Bryant for a few moments on live television. The basketball enthusiast spoke with incredible respect and reverence for his favorite player.

"He is one of the biggest idols in China," says Xinjie. During Bryant's 2013 tour, he recalls, "I saw people stand out on the street outside of his hotel all night. People really love him."[154]

After years of planning and hard work, Xinjie finally opened the Xinjie Sneakerseum in Beijing in 2018. The museum contains signed PEs Bryant wore during historic moments of his career. Incredible stories are told through the hundreds of ultra-rare sneakers: wear-test samples, promo pairs, hybrid sneakers, and mismatched sneakers that were the funny result of miscommunication. Although the museum contains basketball artifacts from other players, it's clear how much of an impact Bryant had on Xinjie's life. What's more, they share the same birthday—August 23.

Preludes, Kobe 9

Like so many times before in Bryant's career, his journey back to the court was nothing short of inspirational. But this time felt different. It was different. Everyone knew his time in the NBA was winding down. That didn't stop the Lakers from signing the perennial All-Star to a two-year contract extension on November 25. Against the odds, Bryant took the court again on December 8 in a home game against the Raptors. To commemorate the moment, Bryant laced up a pair of Kobe 1s in the "Prelude" colorway.

Nike cooked up something special to mark Bryant's return and count down to the release of the Kobe 9. The "Prelude" pack was the first retro of Bryant's signature line. Art, history, and culture went into the elegant colorways. While historic moments of Bryant's career told the stories involved with each sneaker. The self-explanatory names for the pack went: Kobe 1 "81 points," Kobe 2 "4/50+ points,"

Kobe 3 "Misery," Kobe 4 "Finals MVP," Kobe 5 "Finals MVP," Kobe 6 "All-Star MVP," Kobe 7 "London," and Kobe 8 "Reflection." Nike called it the "road to masterpiece." Nike released each sneaker in limited quantities from December of 2013 through January of 2014 for $200.[155]

After playing his first game back in the Kobe 1 "Prelude" colorway, Bryant switched back to wearing Kobe 8 PEs for the next five games. But just six games into his comeback, Bryant suffered a lateral tibial plateau fracture in his left knee. He was initially ruled out for six weeks, then until the All-Star break, before eventually being shut down for the season.[156] The Lakers went 22-55 during the 2013-2014 season, and teammate Nick Young debuted the Nike Kobe 9 Elite.

On December 4, 2013, Nike unveiled the Nike Kobe 9 Elite at the Museum of Contemporary Art (MOCA) in Los Angeles.[157] Designer Eric Avar touted the use of Nike Flyknit and Flywire to create a one-piece upper. The upper materials were innovative, but the internet was more intrigued by the height of the sneaker. Whereas the Kobe 8 was shockingly low, the Kobe 9 Elite went past the ankle and up the shin. It looked like something a boxer would wear in the ring.

Nike said the high ankle collar made of Flyknit created the "proprioceptive feel of a low-top, with the support of a mid-top." In layman's terms, similar to the Kobe 7 System "Attack Strong," the high cut aided in the sensation of knowing the foot's location. It was easy to get caught up in the hype about the upper, but some of the best work took place on the parts you couldn't easily view. The cushion was provided with a full-length, Lunarlon drop-in midsole and a padded inner sleeve that used aero mesh for ventilation. To support the foot, the design team used carbon fiber heel panels rather than a plate under the foot.

The upper was eye-catching, the cushion was adequate, but the outsole made true hoopers happy with the Kobe 9. Based on the pressure mapping of Bryant's feet, the traction pattern looked like a fingerprint. The thin, rubber outsole is still a fan favorite after all these years. Per usual, Nike wasn't shy about branding. A large Swoosh sat on both sides of the foot with the Kobe logo on the giant tongue, and nine stitches ran up the back of the ankle collar to represent the sutures used on Bryant's Achilles. Keeping with tradition, "Kobe Code" dots were imprinted on both sides of the midsole. The code on the lateral side translates to "Masterpiece." The code on the medial side translates to the Latin phrase "Veni, vidi, vici" or "I came, I saw, I conquered" in English.[158]

After seeing the sneaker for the first time in early December of 2013, fans had to wait until February 8, 2014, to get a pair for $225. The commercials for the Kobe 9 Elite continued with the "Masterpiece" theme. The first commercial envisioned Bryant building the "grandest grand masterpieces of grand pianos," before reminding everyone that he didn't create the piano instead of the Kobe 9 collection. An auditorium full of spectators, including Lionel Richie, applauded Bryant. The commercial ended with a shot of the Kobe 9 Elite in the "Perspective" colorway alongside matching clothes from the Nike Kobe line.

The second commercial featured a black mamba made out of Nike Flyknit. The vibrantly colored snake wrapped itself into the Kobe 9 Elite displayed in a painting. A message read "The art of light, strong, and fast" before closing with "Kobe 9 Elite The Masterpiece."[159]

Several artsy colorways took their names from themes and inspirations that were important to Bryant. "All-Star—Maestro," "Details," "Fundamentals," "Hero," "Perspective," "Strategy," and "Victory." Of course, "Black History Month," "Christmas," and "What the Kobe" were all brought back for the Kobe 9 Elite.[160]

Even though the season ended way too early for the Black Mamba, Nike still had more ideas for the signature model. The Kobe 9 released in two different low-cut models. The first and most important was the Kobe 9 Elite Low HTM. HTM was a collaboration of NIKE, Inc. President and CEO Mark Parker, Fragment Design Founder Hiroshi Fujiwara, and Nike Innovation Leader Tinker Hatfield. The HTM collection consisted of four colorways, which released in Milan on April 8.[161] Later that summer, more colorways of the Kobe 9 Elite Low were released, including nods to two of Bryant's favorite musicians with "Beethoven" and "Moonwalker" colorways.

The $200 low-cut model was remarkably similar to the high-top version, sans the proprioceptive collar. The second low-cut model would only cost $160. The Kobe 9 Low EM used Engineered Mesh for its upper rather than Flyknit. Also, TPU was used around the heel rather than the carbon fiber used on both elite models. All three models kept the same cushion and traction pattern.[162]

The Kobe 9 EM used more familiar colorways such as "Bruce

Lee," "China," "Easter," and "USA" alongside some fun, new colorways including "Brazil," "Bright Mango," "Dusty Cactus," "Hypercobalt," "Peach Jam," and "Pop Art."[163] Thanks to NikeiD, fans could customize everything from the laces to the outsoles on both low-cut models. It cost $205 to design the Kobe 9 EM, while changes to the Kobe 9 Elite Low would cost a cringe-inducing $245.[164]

Despite the success of the Nike Kobe line, a troubling trend was developing. Bryant was spending more and more of his summers rehabilitating injuries. As he went, so did the Lakers. The team was in the lottery, not the playoffs. Free agents were opting to play elsewhere, rather than team up with an aging Bryant.

After his knee healed, Bryant resumed his usual whirlwind summer schedule. In June of 2014, he traveled to Brazil for the 2014 FIFA World Cup. Bryant was there to watch the world's best soccer players compete, but more importantly, he was attending Nike events. He loved being around the people and assured everyone his knee was 100% by taking part in a friendly soccer match. Some pretty epic photos and videos exist online of Bryant roaming the streets of Rio in Kobe 9 Elite in the "Gold" colorway and in a Kobe 9 Elite Low "HTM" colorway.[165]

Bryant kept the Kobe 9 Elite Low "HTM" colorways on his feet when he hosted his eighth-annual basketball camp at the University of California, Santa Barbara in July. As always, Bryant was hands-on in the camp, actively passing his basketball knowledge onto another generation. He also took time to field questions from the media about his health status and the future of the Lakers.[166]

On July 20, Bryant met with the family of Trayvon Martin at a rally in Crenshaw, a South Los Angeles neighborhood. The event took place on the one-year anniversary of the day George Zimmerman was acquitted for murdering the 17-year-old Floridian. Bryant spoke to the crowd on the importance of athletes such as himself having a responsibility to use their platform to help the Martin family.[167]

By August, Bryant was deployed to China yet again. The 2014 Nike RISE Basketball campaign marked Bryant's ninth basketball tour in the country. The RISE campaign was a docu-drama that invited young players to compete in front of Nike Basketball's biggest stars and compete for one of three spots in the Nike World Basketball Festival in Barcelona later the following month. With a pair of Kobe 9 Elite Lows in the "University Red" colorway on his feet, Bryant took to the court to work with the young players. Nike went all out with the Shanghai event. The "House of Mamba" featured a full-sized LED basketball court that brought graphics, video, and player-tracking to life. Drills based on Bryant's own training were implemented using the state-of-the-art system.[168]

The 2014-2015 season started by adjusting to another new head coach, former teammate, Byron Scott. After striking out in free agency, the roster consisted mostly of young and inexpensive players. What's more, Bryant had more naysayers than ever. ESPN ranked him as the 40th best player in the NBA. When asked about the ranking, Bryant said, "I've known for a long time they're a bunch of idiots . . . I tend to use things as motivation that tend to be in the realm of reality."[169]

The Lakers started with an abysmal 3-13 record. But that didn't stop Bryant from putting up some monster performances, including a 44-point performance against the Warriors in the Staples Center. He started the season with dazzling Kobe 9 Elite PEs in both the high-top and low-cut models.[170] For the first two months of the season, he played at a high level. Not only was he producing on the court, but he was finding himself outside of basketball.

Bryant used the time while recovering from his Achilles injury to start thinking about life after basketball. His interest in storytelling and problem-solving were the seeds for his post-basketball life. Plus, he was more outspoken on social matters than ever before. On December 10, Bryant and his teammates wore warmup shirts that read, "I CAN'T BREATHE." A New Yorker named Eric Garner recently became the most recent victim of police brutality. A viral video of the moment sparked outrage across the country. The once reserved Bryant began speaking candidly on issues of race, justice, and police brutality.

On December 14, Bryant passed Michael Jordan for third on the NBA All-Time Scoring List. Immediately after sinking the free throws, the referees called a timeout for everyone to recognize the significance of the moment. Bryant walked over and grabbed the game ball before graciously smiling and waving to the Timberwolves fans. For the historic achievement, Bryant wore a pair of Kobe 9 Elite Low PE in a green and purple colorway. Nike quickly released the "Mamba Moment" Kobe 9 Elite Low NikeiD option for a limited time. The green and purple Flyknit upper was a preset, but fans could customize every other facet of the sneaker.[171]

On January 21, 2015, injuries struck again. After sitting out eight of the previous 15 games, Bryant returned with a vengeance against the Pelicans. After throwing down a thunderous jam, Bryant ran back down the court, grabbing at his right shoulder. He attempted to play by only using his left hand before he got pulled from the game. Bryant suffered a rotator cuff tear that required season-ending surgery after just 35 games.

Kobe X

Ten days later, Nick Young would debut the Nike Kobe X. Like its predecessor, the Kobe 10 released in three versions: a low-cut with a mesh upper and both an elite low-cut and elite high-cut with Flyknit uppers. Eric Avar designed the Kobe 10 with a minimalist approach that built on an already solid foundation. The appearance was straight-forward with no frills. A textile-mesh upper with a large Swoosh logo on both sides of the sneaker, and the Kobe logo on the tongue. The left heel counter kept the stitches, while the right heel counter used the Kobe logo.

Most of the innovation occurred out of sight. A hybrid cushioning system used a full-length Lunarlon insole with a large-volume Zoom Air unit under the heel, enhanced by Nike Free inspired flex grooves. The cushioning was contained with rubber sidewalls, which provided support and stability. The advanced traction system lived up to the hype. The soft rubber outsole featured hundreds of "nodules" that gripped the court.[172] The cool part about the setup was how the cushion and traction worked in unison to create maximum court-feel and shock-absorption.

The Kobe 10 released to the public on February 7 for $180. Colorways included familiar themes such as "All Star," "Easter," "Silk," and "USA." New stories were told through "5AM Flight," "Blackout," "Liberty," "Majors," "Overcome," "Pain," and "Vino."[173] The stories told through the colorways represented Bryant's new challenges: injuries, age, and time. Bryant's persona was transforming from a highly skilled assassin to an underdog desperately hanging onto his natural abilities.

On February 21, Nike presented the Kobe X Blackout Experience at The Shrine Expo Hall in Los Angeles. Nike promoted the event as "A fan celebration and artistic expression of the Kobe X." The festivities included music, art, and even a dunk contest. Bryant, with a sling around his right arm, spoke to the media. Serena Williams, a reporter for *LakersNation.com*, asked two pertinent questions that gave fans some insight on Bryant's thoughts about his rabid fan-base.[174]

Williams: Talk about the role your fans have played. The Mamba Army is out here in full force but you go to away games in New York and you go to Miami and people are wearing that Kobe jersey. These fans have been so loyal; what does that mean to you?

Bryant: Well, I think it means more to me than other players who see their jerseys out in the stands 'cause my career has been a long career but we've also been through a lot of stuff, you know, good and bad and all that stuff. So, there's a certain, I think, DNA that we have, a certain mentality that we have, when you're a part of the Mamba Army. It's the understanding that we have with each other that no matter what we go through, we continue to fight through it, right? We continue to battle, we continue to come back on top. So, it means a lot to me to see them representing.

Williams: So, we got the Mamba Army here, you and including myself. You're the commander-in-chief, so what mission do you have for us? What's our challenge?

Bryant: The challenge is the constant to continue to learn, continue to learn, to continue to ask questions, continue to figure things out, continue to ask why things happen a certain way, continue to better yourself, right? 'Cause when that happens you have no choice but to achieve greatness. It comes as a by-product of that. So, continue to challenge yourself.

Two months after the initial release, fans could get their hands on the Nike Kobe 10 Elite. The only major difference from the Kobe 10 that had just released was the Flyknit upper and the proprioceptive collar. The cushioning and traction didn't change at all. One noticeable achievement was the use of recycled polyester yarn in the construction of the Flyknit. Every pair of sneakers was knit with the equivalent of five recycled plastic bottles. The environmentally friendly high-top cost $225.[175]

Nike brought back the polarizing "What the Kobe" colorway but then implemented several clean concepts such as "American," "Commander," "Elevate," and "Rose Gold" along with two Lakers colorways with "Opening Night" in yellow and "Team" in purple.[176]

Lastly, the Kobe 10 Elite Low hit the shelves for $200. Again, not much changed between the two elite models other than the high-top ankle collar. Colorways included "Christmas," "Draft Pick," "Mambacurial," and "Rivalry." Meanwhile, NikeiD let fans go wild with the usual assortment of choices. But special "Grinch," "HTM," "Mambacolor," and "Multicolor" options created the most hype. For the price of $245 fans could reimagine the next-to-last signature sneaker Bryant would wear on the floor.[177]

Commercials for the Kobe 10 were significantly toned down and didn't feature Bryant—or anyone, for that matter. The first ad featured a black mamba slithering around the Kobe 10 before striking. The commercial ended with the message: "Strike With Precision" and "The Kobe X" with the Swoosh logo below it. The second commercial simply spun around the Kobe 10 Elite while displaying its technical features. "Kobe X Elite" appeared on the screen before "Transform Your Game" and "Nike.com/basketball" with the Swoosh logo above the final message.[178]

The Lakers finished the 2014-2015 season with a record of 21-61. Yet again, the team was praying for ping-pong balls to bounce their way in the NBA Draft Lottery. Meanwhile, their highest-paid player was spending another summer rehabilitating a serious injury. There was no doubt Bryant was dedicated to getting back onto the floor and providing his team with the best version of himself. But he was also leaning into his life after basketball.

Bryant balanced his rehab and training regimen with more public appearances for his business ventures and philanthropic interests. In addition to his summer camp in Santa Barbara, Bryant took off for Asia once again. It was his tenth summer tour and second year of the RISE initiative. At every tour stop, he was treated like a conquering hero. Guangzhou August 1-2, Shanghai August 2-4, and Taipei on August 5. Bryant and other Nike Basketball athletes worked hands-on with players of various ages and skill levels for the docu-drama broadcasted in China.[179]

Throughout the tour, Bryant wore one of his lesser-known models, the Nike Kobe Venonmenon 5 in a special PE colorway that reflected China's vibrant culture.[180]

CHAPTER 9

Arrivederci

On August 22, Bryant posted a selfie on his Instagram account. He was back in the Lakers practice facility, wearing sunglasses and smiling ear to ear. The caption read, *"First day back on the court shooting! Bout damn time!! #shoulderrecovery #20thseason @drinkbodyarmor #lakers."*[181]

Bryant was always business minded. In March 2014, he invested in a small sports drink company known as Body Armor for about 10% ownership. Over time he would invest approximately $6 million into Body Armor. By 2018, Coca-Cola became an investor in the company, making Bryant's shares worth an estimated $200 million.[182] So, throughout the 2015-2016 season it wasn't uncommon to see Bryant repping the sports drink company either online or in person.

When October rolled around, it was time for Bryant's 20th season in the NBA. During the preseason, ESPN ranked him as the 93rd best player in the league.[183] They cited his injuries and subpar shooting percentages for the major drop. To make matters worse, ESPN projected the Lakers would only win 27 games.[184] In hindsight, they were far too optimistic. The team would finish the regular season with a

17-65 record. The good news was that Bryant remained healthy for what would be his final year in the NBA.

Years later, teammate Lou Williams shared two stories with the world about Bryant's reaction to a blowout loss against the Trail Blazers in Portland. Williams told the first story on the podcast *All the Smoke* hosted by Matt Barnes and Stephen Jackson. Following the game, Bryant supposedly told his teammates, "From now on out, every time down the court, I touch the ball. Y'all going to learn what it's like to play with Kobe Bean Fucking Bryant." The second story from that disastrous night was shared on Williams's Twitter account. The tweet read, "We got blew out in Portland. He took everybody Kobe's and said they couldn't wear it cause we was soft" followed by two Face with Tears of Joy emojis.[185]

Unrelated to the hilarious Portland stories, and a 2-13 start to the season, Bryant finally shared his retirement plans. The veteran penned an eloquent love letter titled "Dear Basketball" for the publication *The Player's Tribune*. In the heartfelt message, Bryant explained why he had to finally give up the game after playing it his entire life. Fans in attendance at the Staples Center for the November 29 matchup against the Pacers had the sealed letter waiting for them in their seats prior to the game.[186]

The Lakers were in the beginning stages of rebuilding the roster, so the 2015-2016 season's focus shifted to giving the five-time champion a proper sendoff. Bryant's farewell tour was a sight to behold. Large crowds, including fans who traveled from every corner of the globe, packed arenas to see the Black Mamba one final time. As luck would have it, Bryant's first road game after announcing his retirement was in his hometown of Philadelphia. Whereas the 2002 NBA All-Star Game felt like the 1995 Source Awards, the December 1st matchup against the 76ers resembled the 2014 Coachella Festival.

The City of Brotherly Love rolled out the red carpet for their native son. Bryant didn't get the usual monotone introduction of a road team's starter. Instead, the lights went out, and the PA announcer Matt Cord gave a thunderous introduction where he listed Bryant's achievements (including the 1996 State Title for Lower Merion High School).[187] The fans in attendance inside Wells Fargo Center gave resounding applause. Before tip-off, the 76ers organization recognized Bryant. Julius Erving and Bryant's high school coach, Gregg Downer, presented him with a framed Lower Merion jersey with the number

24 (his high school number 33 had already been retired in 2002).

As soon as the game started, Bryant came out gunning. In the first 75 seconds of the game, he made three three-pointers that sent the opposing crowd into a frenzy. As would be the theme for most of the season, the Lakers fell to the 76ers 103-91. Bryant went 7-26 from the field, including 4-17 from behind the arc, and 2-4 from the charity stripe for a total of 20 points.

Shortly after the 76ers lovefest, Bryant requested that opposing teams no longer present him with gifts or ceremonies. A private ceremony or brief video tribute was preferable for the notoriously competitive veteran. Teams followed suit by honoring Bryant during a break in the action with messages or videos on their arena's jumbotrons.[188] Then Bryant would wave goodbye to the opposing crowd one final time.

Lakers Strength and Conditioning Coach Dr. Tim DiFrancesco calls Bryant's entire last season "surreal." He recounted a story from an early-season road trip when players started asking Bryant for his game-worn shoes and getting on a list to request the shoes after each game. "I vividly recall the first game it happened," says DiFrancesco. "We were in Washington, and I believe it was Robert Sacre that was the first to get on that bandwagon. Then everybody, obviously, from one game to the next wanted something game-worn from him [Bryant] all the way down to his final game."[189]

Kobe 11

After starting in the Kobe 10 Elite and Kobe 10 Elite Low in PE colorways, Bryant finally was able to debut his newest signature sneaker himself. The Nike Kobe 11 was unveiled on the app Periscope on December 14 live from the Nike Vault.[190] Visually, not a lot changed with the Kobe 11. It was a low-cut with a large Swoosh logo on the sides that featured a reflective snakeskin pattern. The Kobe logo was placed on the tongue, while stitches remained on the left heel. However, on the right heel, different graphic images told different stories. In the launch colorway called "Achilles Heel," a Trojan warrior image was placed on the right heel to tell the story of the mythological Greek character.

Designer Eric Avar went with an advanced version of Flyknit

technology, which used TPU-yarn that attached directly into the shoe's outsole shell. The rubber outsole was flat with large lateral outriggers. The translucent outsole featured a unique traction pattern with a tread design and clear spine that added additional grip—all of those components coupled with an internal heel counter made for a low-riding, stable sneaker.

For the cushion, the Kobe 11 featured a full-length Lunarlon drop-in midsole with a Nike Zoom Air unit in the heel. Under the forefoot of the midsole, siping grooves allowed for maximum maneuverability. You'll see little Kobe logos on each pod if you look closely enough at the Free-inspired flex grooves. Dense padding around the inside of the ankle collar and tongue provided additional comfort. Bryant debuted the Kobe 11 on December 30 against the Celtics in TD Garden. Fittingly, he went with the purple-and-black colorway called "Eulogy." The Kobe 11 hit shelves on January 9, 2016 for $200.

NikeiD for the Kobe 11 became available to the public on the same day. Fans had more options than ever before—three different drop-in midsoles, multiple outsoles meant for different court surfaces, and numerous icons for an added personal touch. All of those options were impressive, but the Flyknit upper let the public play with different multi-color and gradient designs, which resulted in some fire colorways. The price tag for the ultra-personalized sneaker ranged from $245-$265.[191]

While Bryant consistently brought the heat with PEs in Lakers colorways, Nike kept fans happy with an assortment of general release colorways. "Barcelona" (in both blue and red), "BHM," "Bruce Lee," "Easter," and "USA" were all back in the Kobe 11. New colorways included "Black Space," "Ghost of Christmas Past," "Last Emperor," "Master of Innovation," "Oreo," and the Four Horsemen pack. Bryant gave special colorways as part of his "Muse Pack."[192] Eric Avar, Tinker Hatfield, and Mark Parker all were honored with personalized colorways.

In the final game before the All-Star break, the Lakers traveled to Cleveland to take on the Cavaliers. Following the 120-111 Lakers loss, Bryant reunited with his former Olympic teammate LeBron James to give him a signed pair of his game-worn sneakers, a pair of Kobe 11s in a PE Lakers colorway.[193] The two posed for a picture, which quickly circulated around the internet. It was far from the first or last time that Bryant would give an autographed pair of game-worn kicks to an opposing player.

Baxter Holmes, ESPN Senior Writer, noticed the trend and wrote an in-depth story detailing how NBA players turned into child-like fans around Bryant in his final season. In the article published on March 29, 2016, Bryant estimated that he had given away 30 pairs of signed sneakers to opposing players by that point in the season. On average, Bryant took five pairs of sneakers to each road game, and as many as seven pairs on occasions when he knew there would be a high demand.[194]

Bryant explained in the article that anyone who had the "cojones" to ask would receive a pair of sneakers. Paul George, Trevor Ariza, and Caron Butler were some of the notable players who made the ask. In addition to the autograph, the sneakers often contained a message. The same ESPN article revealed what some of the messages said.

To Draymond Green, Bryant wrote, "Make history!" Bryant must have had a crystal ball because the Warriors had just won the 2015 NBA Finals and won again in 2017 and 2018. Green won the 2017 NBA Defensive Player of the Year.

Tony Allen's message from Bryant read, "To the best defender I ever faced!" Bryant faced many tough defenders, even some who dubbed themselves the "Kobe-stopper." But Allen had battled Bryant in the 2008 and 2010 NBA Finals. Plus, he was named to the NBA All-Defensive First Team in 2012, 2013, and 2015.

Kevin Durant's sneakers read, "Be the greatest." Bryant clearly had high expectations for Durant. Not only did Durant win the 2014 NBA Most Valuable Player Award, but he eventually led the Warriors to two championships in 2017 and 2018. Not to mention, Bryant got a close-up view of what Durant was capable of during the 2012 Olympics in London.

Even though Bryant had requested no more gifts earlier in the season, another legend wasn't going to hear any of that. At a Jordan Brand event on February 12, the brand gifted a complete set of Air Jordans (every model 1-30) in all-white colorways to Bryant. A special nod was given to Bryant's history with Jordan with the Jordan III and Jordan VIII, which featured hints of Lakers purple and gold. Those were two of the Jordan models that Bryant wore during his famed sneaker free-agency season of 2002-2003.

Additionally, a complete set of Air Jordans in all-black colorways were auctioned off on Ebay for charity. The all-black collection in size 14 sold for $240,100. The proceeds split between the Jordan Wings Initiative and the Kobe Bryant and Vanessa Bryant Family Foundation (KVBFF). Jordan Brand President Larry Miller personally presented the gift to Bryant. In a press release, Miller said, "The Jordan Brand is about more than basketball; it's about leaving a legacy and honoring those who have left a legacy." Miller continued, "Tonight, the brand was able to honor one of the game's great players and the legacy he created."[195]

Jeffrey M. Jordan, entrepreneur and head of digital innovation at Jordan Brand, was at the A-List event. Jordan recalled, "That entire weekend was *special*. I remember him [Bryant] having the brightest smile in the room that night. It was freezing in Toronto (it was the coldest temperature I've ever been in as a Chicago native). But the events throughout the weekend had such a warmth that it's hard to describe. But I'll never forget that smile he had, and the aura that followed that weekend."[196]

Toronto hosted the 2016 NBA All-Star Game. Despite being voted to the previous two All-Star games, Bryant was unable to play due to injuries. But in his 18th and final All-Star Game selection, Bryant led the league in fan votes. Before the game, Bryant was honored with a video tribute and a speech given by Magic Johnson. As the crowd chanted "KO-BE," Bryant graciously thanked the fans and league and spoke on his goal of passing on knowledge to the younger players so they could carry on the tradition of the NBA.

In contrast to the simple red-and-white Western Conference uniform, Bryant wore a pair of Kobe 11s in the "All Star—Northern Lights." The loud sneakers featured a black-and-green-glow colorway. The outsole glowed in the dark to mimic the Northern Lights. Fans could scoop up the general release colorway for $220 three days before the game even took place.[197]

After the All-Star festivities in Toronto, the Kobe-mania accelerated into overdrive. Showtime aired the documentary *Kobe Bryant's Muse*. Bryant, the consummate storyteller, was an executive producer, while Gotham Chopra directed the film. *Kobe Bryant's Muse* gives fans a raw, emotional, and candid Bryant. He discussed aspects of his life that he had previously kept to himself. The gritty documentary detailed Bryant's recovery from his Achilles surgery before ending with him receiving the news that he needed shoulder surgery to repair his torn rotator cuff in 2015.

From March 22 to April 13, the "Fade to Black" collection released in limited quantities for $200 per individual pair. The collection marked the second time Bryant's signature sneakers were getting retro treatment. This time the colorways were muted and started with a white Huarache 2K4 and faded to an all-black Kobe 11 with a gold Swoosh logo.[198]

On April 9, Nike released the Kobe 11 EM. As the name indicated, Nike used Engineered Mesh on the upper rather than Flyknit. What consumers lost in durability, they made up for in breathability. Additionally, there was no Zoom Air unit under the heel. But for the most part, the Kobe 11 EM kept much of the same tooling as the Kobe 11 Elite. The budget-friendlier sneaker cost $160.[199]

Nike flooded the market with general release colorways, and fans happily drowned in the wave of Kobe 11 EMs. "3D," "Barcelona" (in bright mango-orange), "Carpe Diem," "Dark Knight," "Draft Day" (including a few with the wrong date on the heel), "Fundamentals," "Invisibility Cloak," "Lower Merion," and "Mambacurial" were all brought back for one last time. New colorways like "Phillipines," "Summer," and "Sunset" were introduced. "Peach Jam," "Quai 54," and "Quai 54 Friends & Family" got special treatment to celebrate the elite basketball tournaments.[200] Additionally, a slew of team bank colorways became available for Nike-sponsored schools.

As Bryant's final game quickly approached, Nike didn't miss the opportunity to air an emotionally charged commercial known as "The Conductor." In the ad, Bryant hits a fadeaway buzzer-beater in Portland, before a fan yells, "Kobe, you suck!" Bryant lifts his hand to his ear as the fans chant, "Kobe sucks!" in unison. Then the lights in the arena go out. A spotlight illuminates Bryant as he points to individual fans in the crowd who begin to sing, "I've been hating you for too long to stop now." An orchestra appears on the court; his former coach Phil Jackson sits at the piano next to Lakers owner Jeanie Buss and continues the song in his baritone voice.

Paul Pierce and Rasheed Wallace stand up and continue the song, while Bryant conducts every note of the love-hate song. Eventually, the entire crowd joins in the chorus, singing, "I hate you—don't make me stop now." Bryant walks off the court while "Just do it" appears on the screen, followed by the Swoosh logo and "#MAMBADAY."[201]

It was officially here. The day so many fans hoped would never arrive. The day so many haters wished would have come sooner. After 20 years, it was Bryant's final game in the NBA. April 13 became known as Mamba Day. Nike named the unofficial holiday and coordinated a massive multimedia tribute to Bryant. In addition to a wave of social media posts and advertisements, Nike enlisted over 200 of its athletes from different sports to wear black-and-gold footwear on the special day. Nike's NBA players recorded video tributes that ranged from somber to hilarious. In Kevin Durant's video, the Thunder star said, "Kobe pissed me off a lot."[202]

Fans could get in on the action too. Once the game tipped off, the Kobe 11 EM "Mamba Day ID" could get customized on NikeiD for a short time. The mesh upper used a graphic that contained eight notable stats from Bryant's career: the dates of his first and last games (11.01.96 and 4.13.16), five World Championships, four All-Star MVP awards, 18 All-Star appearances, 81 points scored in a game, 20 years played in the league, and 24 for his jersey number. People all over the world were able to personalize the sneakers and put their own twist on the bitter-sweet moment. Upper color, Swoosh logo, Kobe logo, laces, accents, outsole, heel graphics, and tongue graphics were all up to the consumer.[203]

With so many options, it was difficult for any two pairs to look alike. Nike included a gold card inside the shoebox that stated "As the stats mounted, so did the love and the hate" and "Love the truth, because numbers don't lie." Additionally, there was an explanation of all numbers used on the upper.[204]

Nike took care of their share of the marketing, while the Lakers threw one of the biggest parties Southern California ever saw. Giant billboards with pictures of Bryant at various stages in his career said, "#THANKYOUKOBE." Whiteboards with translucent photos of Bryant surrounded the arena meant for fans to write personal tributes. The carnival-like atmosphere included a rock-climbing wall, a basketball court, giant inflatables, and balloons as far as the eye can see. For fans lucky (and wealthy) enough to attend the game, a Nike Mamba Day shirt and other collectible items waited for them at their seats. What's more, the team apparel store and Nike Vault offered even more chances for fans to buy rare keepsakes.

Celebrities in attendance included actors like Jack Nicholson, Brian Austin Green, Josh Hutcherson, O'Shea Jackson Jr., and Zendaya.

Musicians such as Kanye West, Snoop Dogg, Jay Z, Kendrick Lamar, ScHoolboy Q, The Weeknd, G-Eazy, and Paula Abdul were in full force.

Naturally, models like Bella Hadid and Behati Prinsloo were at the star-studded event. Comedians Arsenio Hall and George Lopez had good seats. Many former Lakers were scattered all over the place, not to mention soccer star David Beckham. Music executives like Anthony Tiffith and countless other titans of industry all made their way to Staples Center to pay homage to the man who had given them so much of himself for two decades.[205]

To the surprise of no one, a lengthy pregame ceremony took place. A touching video tribute followed by a speech from Magic Johnson ensured everyone watching would be emotional. Finally, after all the hoopla, it was time for the game to start. What ensued was a legendary Black Mamba experience that rocked the basketball world. In just over 42 minutes, Bryant poured in 60 points. Sure, it was on 22 of 50 shot attempts, but no one cared about efficiency that night. That sort of output seemed unfathomable for a 37-year-old with so many miles logged on his body. With each shot, the crowd got louder and louder before eventual pandemonium when he hit his final free throw to secure the highest-scoring game by a player of his age.

Analytics nerds and hot-take artists saw the game as the perfect example as to why Bryant was overrated. But they were blinded by their calculators. Games were never about percentages and efficiency rates with Bryant. For Bryant, each game was a war of attrition. His prolific volume of shooting was intended to wear down defenders both physically and mentally. Not every shot was a knockout blow, but he kept slicing at teams until they died a death by a thousand cuts.

Following the 101-96 win over the Jazz, Bryant walked to center court to give the fans one last farewell. With a Body Armor towel around his shoulders and a pair of sweat-soaked Kobe 11 "Fade to Black" sneakers on his feet, Bryant thanked the fans. His final words of the speech were "Mamba out" before dropping the mic on the floor. The phrase "Mamba out" quickly became a popular phrase. Even President Barack Obama said, "Obama out" in his final White House Correspondent's Dinner a few weeks later.

After Bryant made his way through the crowd to the locker room, champagne waited on the team. Players lined up to get something, anything, autographed by Bryant following his iconic final game.

Years later, Nick Young told his story following the game on the *Certified Buckets* podcast. Young, who had once debuted the Kobe 9 and Kobe 10, had since signed a deal with Adidas in December of 2015. He approached Bryant with some of his old sneakers, formerly known as the KB8, but since renamed the Crazy 8 since Adidas re-released the sneaker in 2015. According to Young, Bryant said, "I ain't signing these shits" and threw the Adidas sneakers in the trash. Luckily, Young was able to get a pair of Nike Kobes and the scoresheet signed.[206]

At long last, the snake had shed his skin and was ready to begin the next phase of his life.

CHAPTER 10

Rebirth

Bryant never even entertained the possibility of going back to basketball after retiring. He dedicated himself to his family and pursuing his interests in business and storytelling. But what about his signature sneaker line? What about his future with Nike? Luckily, Bryant assured fans that his Nike line wasn't going anywhere. That was evident when the "Nike Mamba Mentality Tour" kicked off in June of 2016 and covered multiple countries in Europe.[207] The next month, the former Laker made a trip to Asia where he did everything from hosting basketball clinics to hanging out with Buddhist monks in Taiwan.[208]

Bryant's post-basketball life got even better with the news of a third child on the way. On July 12, Bryant broke the news on his personal Instagram account. The photo pictured a onesie that read "BABY MAMBA" with a red bow and baby Kobe 11s in the "Achilles Heel" colorway.[209] Kobe and Vanessa's third girl, Bianka, was born approximately five months later on December 5.

Important milestones in late summer and early fall of 2016 continued to keep Bryant busy. On August 22, Bryant and his partners in the investment platform Bryant-Stibel rang the opening bell on the New York Stock Exchange.[210] The following day on August 23, Bryant celebrated his 38th birthday with his family. Then, on August 24, the City of Los Angeles hosted the Bryant family as they declared the day (8/24) to be "Kobe Bryant Day." Although the date was a nod to his two jersey numbers, the honor had just as much to do with Kobe and Vanessa's philanthropy.[211] The Kobe and Vanessa Bryant Family Foundation had long been dedicated to improving the lives of youth and families in need and encouraging young people to stay active through sports.

Only the Black Mamba's schedule could be this hectic during retirement.

On September 16, the video game NBA 2K17 released worldwide. Bryant graced the Legend Edition cover, which cost $80, and Legend Edition Gold for $100. Both versions of the video game came with more perks than the Standard Edition that featured Paul George on the cover for $60.[212]

Kobe A.D.

Sneakerheads everywhere were relieved when images of a shoe rumored to be the "Kobe 12" started popping up online. However, the Kobe 1 through 11 would stand alone, and a new series created. Nike hosted an event for the newest sneaker on November 1, also known as Día de los Muertos, or Day of the Dead. The celebration felt more like a funeral than a party, and that was intentional. Inside a dimly lit warehouse in Los Angeles known as the "Mamba Gallery," candles surrounded by flowers sat on the floor and sugar skulls hung from the walls. Even a funeral guestbook that was meant to be signed by all who attended was on a podium near the entrance.[213] Bryant sat down with YouTube personalities and reporters from various websites to discuss everything from sneakers to retirement to death.

Keeping with the morbid theme, the first sneaker for Bryant after retirement was called the Nike Kobe A.D. Of course, the A.D. stood for "after death." After months of speculation, the public finally got to see the model and break down the tech specs. The Kobe A.D. featured a textile mesh upper that incorporated Dynamic Flywire, which resulted in plenty of durability and support. Besides the Swoosh logos on the sides and the Kobe logo on the tongue, the most eye-catching part of the sneaker was the metallic external heel cup that provided support. An encapsulated Lunarlon midsole with a small Zoom Air unit under the heel provided a little cushion with a lot of court feel. The rubber outsole integrated two different traction patterns—the forefoot resembled the Kobe 10 "nodules," while the heel looked like the snakeskin used in the Kobe 6. Fans were able to pick up the Kobe A.D. on November 22 for $160.[214]

On the same day as the launch colorway known as "Ruthless Precision," NikeiD allowed fans to begin customizing the new model. The options were significantly limited compared to when Nike went all out for the Kobe 11. Therefore, the price was a lot more palatable. It would only cost fans $205 to design their own pairs of Kobe A.D.s.

Nike also cut way back on the number of colorways produced for the Kobe A.D. Familiar colorways such as the "Black Mamba," "Big Stage," and "Black History Month" were back. With the exception of the black-and-yellow "Oregon" colorway that featured a duck-feather graphic, most of the colorways stuck with basic names that reflected the colors on the upper. The "Black White," "Chrome," "Igloo," "Light Bone," "Purple Stardust," "Midnight Navy," and "University Red" all looked sharp, but did little storytelling.[215]

What storytelling the Kobe A.D. lacked was made up for in Bryant's new short-form video series for ESPN. Bryant created, wrote, and directed six videos that focused on various aspects of basketball. The Disney-esque series called *Canvas* premiered on the pregame show *NBA Countdown* before the Christmas Day game between the Warriors and Cavaliers.[216] It continued to air before marquee matchups on both ABC and ESPN throughout the remainder of the 2016-2017 season. The project's goal was to create entertaining short videos that simplified basketball concepts that the whole family could enjoy. Puppets, animations, and musical compositions taught children about off-ball movement and defensive positioning. *Canvas* was as successful as it was ambitious. There was no doubt that Bryant had a bright future outside of basketball and shoe sales.

Now that Bryant was no longer in the league, who would wear Nike Kobes? The answer—a lot of players. DeMar DeRozan had always been a fan of Bryant and his footwear, so naturally, the Raptors guard was the torchbearer of the Kobe line. He got several PEs, including a pair known as the "Compton" colorway that released to the public on April 12, 2017. The pale-gray sneaked had a purple, orange, and blue Kobe logo on the tongue that referenced Bryant's airball against the Jazz in 1997. The insole featured the streets of Compton, with "City of Compton" printed under the heel.[217]

Another NBA player who made history in the Kobe A.D. was Isaiah Thomas of the Celtics. Thomas stood at 5'9" and was the last pick of the 2011 NBA Draft. He embodied the Mamba Mentality. In 2017, Thomas averaged 28.9 points and 5.9 assists per game, while leading the Celtics to the playoffs. The day before the Celtics faced the Bulls in the first round, his sister Chyna Thomas died in a one-car accident. Isaiah was visibly shaken during the pregame warmups and decided to play through the emotional pain and scored 33 points. On his pair of green-and-black Kobe A.D. PEs, he wrote his sister's name and "R.I.P. Lil Sis," "I Love You," and "4-5-17."[218] Thomas carried the Celtics on his back to the Eastern Conference Finals against the Cavaliers until he had to miss the remainder of the series with a serious hip injury.

Jarrel Harris, NBA and Sneakers Editor for *Sports Illustrated*, has had a front-row seat for players wearing the Kobe A.D.. "The Kobe A.D. line was a brilliant strategy to prepare for the next phase of Kobe's signature line after his retirement. He was a big influence on this generation's players. Players like DeMar DeRozan, Jewell Lloyd, Sabrina Ionescu, Isaiah Thomas, Giannis Antetokounmpo, Jayson Tatum, and Devin Booker viewed him as their Michael Jordan. The A.D. line was created to give them the torch and to carry on his legacy."

Harris added important context by recalling Bryant's exact words. "This quote from Kobe in the news release of the Kobe A.D. pretty much sums up everything: 'Even though I am not on the court every day, there are people around the world who are helping to keep the Mamba Mentality alive. I have seen it in basketball, football, and with everyday individuals who are working to be better and are committed to being great.'"[219]

In addition to professional players, the Kobe sneaker line was regularly worn by Angelinos. Harrison Faigen, editor-in-chief and senior producer for *Silver Screen & Roll*, points to the shoes' ability to be worn on and off the court. Faigen explains, "Kobes are the go-to basketball shoes at most basketball games I have ever been to, organized or not. Whether it's how well they work or just his popularity (or both), it is clear that he definitely got a ton of people in Los

Angeles to wear them. They are also by far the basketball shoe (other than the Air Jordan 1, which is more of a lifestyle shoe at this point) that I see people wear the most off the court."[220]

Kobe A.D. NXT, Kobe A.D. Mid

The spring of 2017 also saw the release of the Nike Kobe A.D. NXT. Designer Eric Avar worked with Bryant to once again redefine the look and feel of a basketball sneaker. The most obvious change came in the form of a new lacing structure. There was no way to tie these shoes since they could only be tightened or loosened using a tiny plastic lace lock—the lacing system wrapped over the top of the foot and hidden from view under a shroud.[221] The one-piece Flyknit upper worked in tandem with the lacing structure to keep the foot secure and locked into place. The fit was so snug a pull tab was sewn onto the heel to help get the sneaker on and off.

The tongue of the sneaker, also hidden under the shroud, used Nike Torch technology to add even more ventilation and breathability. Keeping with the light-weight design, the cushion was provided by a drop-in Lunarlon midsole with a Zoom Air unit under the heel (almost identical to the Kobe 11 setup).[222] The translucent rubber outsole kept the same traction pattern as the Kobe A.D.. Branding included a Swoosh logo on both sides of the midsole, a Kobe logo on the right heel, and stitches on the left heel. The Kobe A.D. NXT remained true to the Kobe line's vision by keeping a low-profile, minimalist design. The global release date was April 3 for a price of $200.

As would be the case with the NXT versions of the Kobe A.D. line, there would be no customization on NikeiD. Additionally, not many colorways were released. Only "Black White," "Mambacurial," "Snow White," "University Red," "Volt," and "Wolf Grey" would get released to the public.[223]

Despite no longer playing in the league, Bryant's sneaker line remained the preferred choice of NBA players. *Versus Reviews* published a report that found more NBA players wore Kobes than any other sponsored shoe during the 2016-2017 season. Fifty-eight players in the league wore Kobes, with 33 of them wearing the Kobe

A.D..[224] Luckily for heirs to the Black Mamba, Nike and Bryant had more heat coming soon.

During the 2017 Drew League, the newest Kobe sneaker popped up on the feet of a player. Social media and message boards lit up, not only because it was yet another new Kobe, but because of its appearance. On August 14, Nike introduced what they called "the all-new, mid-top Kobe A.D." The sneaker was widely referred to as the Kobe A.D. Mid. Not only did Nike introduce the new model, but they previewed five general release colorways.

Rather than traditional storytelling, these colorways were built on the psychology of color. An all-purple colorway called "Fearless" represented overcoming challenges and setting fresh goals. "Passion" was naturally an all-red colorway. The all-yellow colorway known as "Optimism" was inspired by the sun and Bryant's supreme self-belief. The all-gray "Detached" colorway represented calm neutrality. Lastly, "Honesty" was depicted by an all-blue colorway that relayed dependability and trust, which Bryant equated with honesty.[225]

The Kobe A.D. Mid was a major departure from the Kobe A.D.. The mid-cut sneaker used a synthetic upper that mimicked suede or felt. The cushion improved by using a full-length Lunarlon midsole and large-volume Zoom Air unit under the heel. A heavily padded ankle collar helped make up for a paper-thin tongue. Support was provided by an internal heel counter, lateral outriggers, and a carbon fiber plate in the shape of the Kobe logo under the foot. The flat outsole used soft rubber in a multi-directional pattern, which provided excellent traction.

Branding was all over the Kobe A.D. Mid. The Swoosh logo was on both sides of the foot, Kobe's signature was sewn into the tongue on the left foot, and the Kobe logo was sewn into the tongue on the right foot. In most colorways, the Kobe logo was on the right heel, with Kobe Code on the left heel. However, the designs on the heel changed with certain colorways to tell different stories.

The Kobe A.D. Mid was released on August 24 (8/24 was a nod to his jersey numbers) for $150.[226]

On the same day, Bryant took to social media to post photos that served as challenges to athletes and even rapper Kendrick Lamar.[227]

At 11:32 a.m.: "#MambaMentality" with an image that read "ANY QUESTIONS. CALL ME. 1-833-KOBE824" and the Kobe logo just below the phone number.

At 12:33p.m.: "@Isaiah_Thomas I challenge you to make the All-NBA First Team next season #MambaMentality." An accompanying image reads "FEARLESS" in purple.

At 12:48 p.m.: "@DeMar_DeRozan I challenge you to rekindle a lost friendship from your youth in Compton #MambaMentality". An accompanying image reads "HONESTY" in blue.

At 1:00 p.m.: "@KenrickLamar I challenge your record label to revolutionize the music program at Centennial High School #MambaMentality." An accompanying image reads "DETACHED" in gray.

At 1:15 p.m.: "@allysonfelix I challenge you to coach the sprinters for the upcoming Special Olympics #MambaMentality." An accompanying image reads "PASSION" in red.

At 1:30 p.m.: "@R_Sherman25 I challenge you to break the Seahawks single season interception record #MambaMentality." An accompanying image reads "OPTIMISM" in yellow.

Giannis Antetokounmpo wanted in on the action and asked Bryant for a challenge on twitter that day, then again three days later. Finally, Bryant responded by quoting the tweet and replying with "MVP."[228] Antetokounmpo went on to win the NBA Most Valuable Player Award the season after in 2019. After Antetokounmpo won the award, somewhere, Bryant probably said, "You're welcome" and "You can do better, I know you can. Good luck to you, Giannis Antetokounmpo."

By October of 2017, fans could customize their own pair on NikeiD. Upper colors, heel graphics, and a multitude of outsole options were available online for $180.[229] For those who didn't want to spend the extra $30 for customization, Nike released rolled out a steady flow of general release colorways. Several energy colorways such as "Baseline," "Black Gum," "Port Wine," "Pure Platinum," and "Rise" hit the shelves, not to mention a plethora of team bank colorways for Nike-sponsored schools.[230]

But a few colorways stood out among the rest. A black-and-gold pair was released to match the alternate Lakers "City Edition" uniforms. The "NCAA Tournament" colorway featured a confetti-inspired outsole with an iridescent Swoosh logo. A blue DeMar DeRozan PE featured more premium materials, including a snakeskin upper and an insole that pictured both Derozan and Bryant. A purple-and-orange Devin Booker PE colorway honored the Suns guard with pictures of his face in the Swoosh logo. Former Celtic

Isaiah Thomas got a PE dubbed "Mighty IT" in a red colorway, which included a shrunken Swoosh logo and a chip in the tongue to resemble a chipped tooth Thomas had suffered while playing.[231]

As for Bryant himself, he remained busier than ever. In October 2017, he went to Paris as an ambassador for Nike. Aside from his events, Bryant visited the Paris St. Germain practice facility and kicked it with Neymar. On December 18, the Lakers officially retired both of his numbers, 8 and 24. Magic Johnson and Jeanie Buss stood at half court and addressed the sold-out Staples Center crowd. Then the spotlight shined on the rafters, as two Bryant jerseys were revealed (one on both sides of the retired jersey for announcer Chick Hearn). With his family looking on, Bryant thanked the organization and fans and expressed optimism for the next 20 years for the Lakers. Of course, he ended his speech with "Mamba out" as the crowd erupted.[232]

Leading up to the retirement of both numbers, Nike fueled the excitement by bringing out some old friends. The MVPuppets were back and better than ever. In three thirty-second commercials, the self-absorbed Kobe puppet continuously annoyed the ever-patient LeBron puppet as they relaxed on the beach. Throughout the three videos, the Kobe puppet lectured the LeBron puppet on each jersey's two personas, the debate between the jersey numbers, and how the Kobe puppet saved the LeBron puppet from the incredible burden of having two jerseys retired.[233]

On January 12, 2018, Bryant announced a new show with ESPN titled *DETAIL*. In each episode, Bryant chose a specific player or team in the NBA and analyzed different aspects of their game. Not only was the show successful, but it eventually expanded to include Peyton Manning and other hosts.[234] *DETAIL* was one of many successful projects to come from Granity Studios, founded by Bryant. Bryant continued to reach success at success at success. On March 4, he won an Oscar for his retirement-letter-turned-short-film, known as *Dear Basketball*. The executive producer took home more hardware; this time, it was for best animated short film.[235] Bryant had proven he was capable of succeeding in industries besides basketball. Trophy in hand and beautiful wife by his side, Bryant was truly a happy man.

Protros, More A.D.'s

Sneakerheads were happy for Bryant and especially happy with the release of the Nike Zoom Kobe 1 Protro. It all started with a cryptic tweet on February 5, 2018. He asked what the word "Protro" meant and promised a special prize to whoever was the first to reply with the correct answer. We soon found out that "Protro" was a combination of the words "performance" and "retro."[236] Bryant said numerous times that he wasn't a fan of retroing his old sneakers, insisting that his line stood for progress and evolution. Luckily for fans, the Protro series did just that.

The Kobe 1 Protro released on February 17 for $175. The performance upgrades were more than just lip service. A full-length Zoom Air unit and thinner Phylon midsole made the sneaker more comfortable without sacrificing any court feel. The carbon fiber plate in the Kobe 1 Protro was nearly half the size as the plate used in the Kobe 1, which made for better heel-to-toe transition and a less clunky sneaker.[237] The Kobe 1 Protro was nearly five ounces lighter than the original, making it a popular choice among NBA players. Devin Booker, DeMar DeRozan, Buddy Hield, and Kyle Kuzma were just a few of the several players who laced up the Kobe 1 Protro on the court.

Although the Kobe 1 Protro was never made available on NikeiD, Nike released several OG colorways and PEs. "81 Points," "All-Star," "Black Out," "Del Sol," "Final Seconds," "MPLS," and "USA" were all brought back, while new colorways garnered even more attention, such as the "Devin Booker PE," "DeMar DeRozan PE," "Mamba Day," and "Noise Cancelling." The boutique Undefeated (UNDFTD) teamed up with Nike to drop several colorways that were as hyped up as they were limited.[238]

Jarrel Harris, NBA and Sneakers Editor for *Sports Illustrated*, says, "Leave it to Kobe to coin a new term 'Protro' to describe his retro line. He wasn't a fan of releasing a retro line but gave in with one condition: he was able to elevate it with the newest tech. He worked on the Zoom Kobe 1 Protro for three years before the announcement."

Looking forward, Harris says, "There are just so many ways Nike can go with the Protro line. I think it is pretty cool that we are seeing new colorways and modifications of some classic sneakers. PJ Tucker is a big Kobe sneaker guy and hasn't been shy about unveiling new concepts. DeMar DeRozan and Devin Booker are also carrying his legacy each game they wear Protro models."[239]

Just in time for the 2017-2018 NBA season's final stretch, Nike and Bryant shocked the sneaker world with the most innovative basketball sneaker to date. On March 21, DeMar DeRozan debuted the Nike Kobe A.D. NXT 360. Nike used its next generation Flyknit to completely wrap the foot with 360-degree construction. A nearly transparent outsole used incredibly thin rubber with an aggressive multi-directional traction pattern that grabbed the court. Cushion for the minimalist sneaker was provided by a drop-in midsole that incorporated React under the heel and Lunarlon under the forefoot.[240] A sculpted heel cup kept the foot secure and promoted maneuverability.

It didn't matter the quality of the TV in your home; it was easy to tell the new sneaker on DeRozan's feet was a Kobe. A large Swoosh logo on the sneaker's lateral side, a Kobe logo on the tongue and right heel, and stitches on the left heel. On the outsole, two different colors created the appearance of a snake sliding up the center of the sneaker. The Nike Kobe A.D. NXT 360 was the quintessential Kobe model. It used ground-breaking technology and looked more like a soccer cleat than a basketball sneaker. The nearly see-through sneaker weighed just over 11 ounces. Fans could get their hands on the Kobe A.D. NXT 360 for $200 on April 13 (Mamba Day).

As was the case with the Kobe A.D. NXT, the colorways for the Kobe A.D. NXT 360 were very limited. No NikeiD treatment, and fans could choose from only a few colorways: "Black Multicolor," "Infrared," "Mamba Day," "Multicolor," "White Multicolor," and "Yellow Strike," which resembled a Lakers colorway.[241]

If for some reason the Kobe 1 Protro and the Kobe A.D. NXT 360 didn't appeal to fans, they would get a glimpse of another new model at the 2018 Drew League. On August 11, DeMar DeRozan wore a pair of the new Kobes. The following day, Bryant and his daughter, Gianna, sat courtside for the Championship Game. As always, everyone's eyes were on Kobe's feet, and he was wearing the same new sneakers that DeRozan had worn the day prior.

On August 24 (Kobe Day, not to be confused with Mamba Day), the Nike Kobe AD released for $140.[242] Yes, you read that right—that was the name Nike gave the newest model. There were no periods between the "A" and the "D" this time. The model quickly became known as the Kobe AD Exodus to keep things from getting even more confusing. Depending on who you ask, the name "Exodus" came from either the first colorway or an image on the Foot Locker release calendar.

Semantics aside, the Kobe AD Exodus used different materials and layering on its one-piece bootie upper. The back panel used the synthetic felt-like material previously seen on the Kobe A.D. Mid, while the toe box used a breathable light-weight mesh. The tongue provided even more ventilation, which looked to have used a version of Nike Torch technology. The felt rear and mesh toe box were married by a flex zone made of composite fiber that wrapped over the top of the forefoot.

The cushion was provided by an injected-Phylon midsole with a Zoom Air unit under the heel, which covered far more space than the Zoom Air unit used in the Kobe A.D. Mid. The soft rubber outsole improved by using a toned-down and more durable version of the Kobe A.D. NXT 360's traction pattern. The carbon fiber plate used by the Kobe A.D. Mid was gone, which resulted in a much more flexible sneaker.[243] A wide forefoot, lateral outriggers, a pair of internal and external heel counters aided in overall support.

Branding included the Swoosh logo on the lateral side with an oversized Kobe logo on the medial side of the foot. The Kobe logo was stitched into the front pull tab and left heel. "KBB" was stitched into the interior side of the front pull tab. Breaking from tradition, the right heel spelled out "K-O-B-E" in a square design. Kobe Code sat below the external heel counter. Sewn-in fabric lace locks featured the numbers "08," "23," and "78" (Bryant's birthday) on the right sneaker, while the left lace locks used the numbers "33," "8," and "24" (Bryant's high school and pro jersey numbers, respectively).

NikeiD was available online for $160 with modest customization options.[244] However, the different materials used in the Kobe AD Exodus made for some unique custom colorways. Little to no storytelling took place with general release colorways. But Nike did flood the market with more than enough energy colorways to fit whatever mood fans were feeling. Additionally, team bank colors were readily available and seen on the feet of college players at Nike-sponsored schools.

While Kobe-fanatics emptied their wallets on the steady stream of new sneakers, Bryant continued to grab important achievements like they were rebounds. On October 23, Bryant's first book titled *The Mamba Mentality: How I Play* was released and quickly consumed by his fan base. In December of 2018, he announced the first of many young adult novels from Granity Studious, titled *The Wizenard Series: Training Camp*. In that same month, he announced the Mamba Sports Academy, a multi-sport training facility for young athletes.

   Before the end of 2018, Bryant sat down for the Barstool Sports podcast *The Corp with A-Rod and Big Cat*. A comfortable and easy-going Bryant matched with unafraid and well-informed hosts made for some excellent content. Nearing the end of the interview, Big Cat looked at his yellow legal pad of notes and rattled off several questions most fans would never dream of asking Bryant if they got the chance to speak with him. What resulted was some funny and honest answers from the notoriously private Bryant.

   Big Cat asked, "Your 2000 rap album—were you just like, 'Fuck it, I can do anything'?"

   Bryant responded with a laugh and said, "It was poetic. Nah, it wasn't that bad. The album itself wasn't that bad. But it taught me how to write."

   The conversation then switched to sneakers. Big Cat asked, "The Kobe 2s. The worst shoe of all time."

   Bryant was confused by the statement in the form of a question. "Which ones?" (Keep in mind, multiple versions of the Nike Kobe 2 released). "The Nike ones?"

   Big Cat pulled out a picture on his iPhone of the Adidas Kobe 2 and showed it to Bryant.

   "The other company? Oh, those don't count!" said Bryant.

   Big Cat, barely containing his laughter, reiterated that they count over Bryant's objections.

   Waving his hand to dismiss it, Bryant said, "That's what taught me I need to lead the design charge."

   Undaunted, Big Cat pressed Bryant on the 2010 *LA Times Magazine* "White Hot" photoshoot, followed by a question about the 2002 Western Conference Finals against the Kings being "rigged."

   Bryant answered both questions with hilarious but honest answers. Without wanting to give away the whole episode, it is worth watching on YouTube.[245] There are some real gems and Easter eggs scattered throughout the wide-ranging interview.

Kobe and Vanessa kicked off the new year by announcing on January 1, 2019 they were expecting a fourth daughter (Capri Kobe Bryant was born later that year on June 20). The following month, Nike and Bryant gave fans more reason to celebrate by releasing the Nike Zoom Kobe IV Protro. The sneaker that started the low-cut craze in 2009 was back again. It's hard to improve upon a near-perfect model. Nike touted an adjusted vamp shape, sleeker heel shape, and wider outsole traction in the Kobe 4 Protro.[246] It truly is a testament to how impressive the sneaker was in 2009 that very few changes were made in 2019, and it was still a performance beast.

It was available on February 15 for $175. Like the Kobe 1 Protro, there was no customization option on NikeiD. And to the dismay of fans, even fewer general release colorways hit the shelves. "Draft Day" made perfect sense for the launch colorway. The 2019 NBA All-Star Game took place in Charlotte and it was a good opportunity to remind younger fans the Hornets drafted Bryant in 1996. Two more OG colorways came with: the "Carpe Diem" and "Del Sol—POP."

Bryant's final season was honored with the "FTB" colorway. A wild upper on the "Wizenard" colorway gave a nod to Bryant's new novel series. As always, the most-hyped Kobe 4 Protros came from Undefeated (UNDFTD). They released five colorways: "Black Mamba," "Court Purple," "Hyper Jade," "Fir," and "Team Orange." The "Hyper Jade" colorway was a PE for DeMar DeRozan who had been traded to the Spurs. The "Fir" colorway was a PE Giannis Antetokounmpo of the Bucs, who wore Kobes before getting his own signature sneaker with Nike (Nike Zoom Freak). "Team Orange" was a PE for Devin Booker of the Suns.[247]

NBA players tantalized fans with the array of Kobe 4 Protro PEs they trotted out in 2019 and 2020. In addition to the players who carried the Kobe torch, Trevor Ariza, Alex Caruso, Anthony Davis, Luka Doncic, Tobias Harris, Kyle Kuzma, Paul Millsap, Malik Monk, Ja Morant, and PJ Tucker all got PE colorways that never released to the public. But it wasn't just NBA players carrying on Kobe's sneaker legacy. WNBA players including Essence Carson, Epiphany Prince, Kristi Toliver, and Tamera Young were just a few players from the league who had an affinity for the Kobe 4 Protro.

Meredith Cash, Sports Reporter for *Business Insider*, put the importance of the sneakers into a historical perspective. Cash said, "There hasn't been a WNBA signature shoe since Candace Parker's Ace3 came out in 2012, and Nike hasn't released one on the women's side since Diana Taurasi's Nike Shox DT dropped in 2006, so even the WNBA's brightest stars wear NBA kicks. Kobes are amongst the most popular sneakers worn by Nike-sponsored players."[248]

Following the release of the Kobe 4 Protro, Bryant continued to make headlines. In March of 2019, Kobe, his daughter Gianna, and the rest of their AAU team were on the cover of *SLAM* magazine.[249] The magazine's cover story detailed Bryant's life after basketball, including stories of how he coached his daughter and her teammates. The entire piece was nothing short of heart-warming. Hearing anecdotes on how the notoriously competitive player passed his knowledge onto the youngest generation of basketball players felt like a dream fulfilled.

CHAPTER 11

#GirlDad

In fact, Bryant was living the dream. He spent the spring and summer of 2019 spending quality time with his family and promoting new projects developing from Granity Studios. Despite a busy schedule that involved interviews, appearances, and travel, Bryant wasn't sacrificing time with his young family. He was still attending volleyball matches, making dates with wife, and carving out time for the occasional social media post about the hit HBO TV show *Game of Thrones*.

On August 22, 2019, Nike put a well-produced video on their YouTube channel titled, "Kobe Bryant: Don't Change Your Dreams | Birthplace of Dreams | Nike."[250] In the video, Bryant, wearing a black long-sleeve shirt with the Mamba logo on the chest, sits in front of the camera and discusses the importance of investing in children. Upbeat music plays while clips roll of kids playing basketball in the Mamba League.

Bryant concludes the video by saying, "My hope is that through sport they understand that whatever discipline they decide to go into—whether it is volleyball or basketball, or whether it's being an accountant or being a writer or whatever the case may be—the same principles apply. The discipline, the dedication, the attention to detail, the unselfishness—all that stuff is there. So hopefully, they grow up understanding that message."

Two days later it was time for Nike and Bryant to unleash their newest creation on the world. The Nike Kobe AD NXT, often referred to as the Kobe AD NXT FastFit, so as not to be confused with the model from 2017. Similar to the Air Jordan 33, the Kobe AD NXT FastFit didn't use a traditional lacing system. Nike FastFit requires only a single tug on the forefoot strap, which activates a pulley system consisting of cables (similar to parachute cords) to tighten the shoe and evenly secure the foot into place. Nike FastFit allows athletes just to pull a side loop to eject out of the shoe rather than untying.

Lockdown had always been an important component of Kobe's signature line, but it was the calling card for this model. In addition to the FastFit system, an ankle strap wraps over the tongue to provide additional support. Meanwhile, underneath a super-thin synthetic upper, an internal mesh bootie known as Nike Quadfit conforms to the foot.[251]

A full-length React drop-in midsole provides adequate cushion. A heavily padded ankle collar provides additional comfort. A rubber outsole features a new multi-directional traction pattern designed specifically for indoor courts. Lateral outriggers and an external heel counter aid in stability and support for the minimalist sneaker.

As if there was any doubt regarding the brand or signature athlete this futuristic sneaker belonged to, there is ample branding. A large transparent Swoosh logo sits on the lateral side of the foot. The Kobe Logo is on the tongue, the ankle strap, and the center of the outsole. Bryant's signature discretely appears on the lateral side of the heel plus, stitches on the pull tab of the left sneaker.

A lot of new technology went into this model—React, FastFit, and Quadfit. All the different ingredients worked together in harmony. In Nike's press release on August 8, Ross Klein, Senior Creative Director for Nike Basketball Footwear, said, "It is our most technologically advanced basketball shoe we've done in the KOBE line, due to the combination of complex components."[252]

Kobe AD NXT FastFit dropped on August 24 (Kobe Day) for $200. Unfortunately, there was no NikeiD option available to fans. Further complicating matters, there were only four general release colorways: "Blue Hero," "Multi-Color," "Off-Noir," and "Vast Grey."[253] Any detractors of the sneaker's appearance were quickly silenced by the abundance of NBA players who enjoyed the newest edition of the AD NXT. OG Anunoby, Anthony Davis, Cheick Diallo, Shai Gilgeous-Alexander, Josh Hart, Dwight Howard, Ja Morant, and Eric Paschall were just a few of the many players who took to the court of Kobe AD NXT Fastfit.

With the new sneaker came a new basketball season. Bryant continued to manage a hectic business schedule without sacrificing time with his family. It was more evident than ever that his daughter, Gianna, had a bright future in basketball. In fact, Gianna's love for the game helped bring Kobe back to the game. Not only was he was coaching her AAU team, but the two were attending NBA games every chance they got through the first few months of the 2019-2020 season.

On November 17, the two attended a game between the Lakers and Hawks at the Staples Center. In a funny reversal of roles, Kobe was asked to hold the camera as his daughter got pictures with her favorite celebrities—Offset and Quavo of the rap group Migos and comedian Kevin Hart.[254] On December 21, a video of Kobe and Gianna went viral after they attended a game at the Barclays Center in Brooklyn between the Nets and Hawks. In the video, Kobe explains something they see on the court. You can see the wheels turning in Gianna's mind before she finishes her father's sentence, and Kobe's eyes light up with pride.[255]

Just over a week later, on December 28, the two sat front row for a game between the Lakers and Mavericks at the Staples Center. In the third quarter, Mavericks guard Luka Doncic walked to the sideline to inbound a pass when he was heckled in Slovenian. It was none other than Kobe himself. He was wearing a bright orange WNBA hoodie and green Eagles toboggan, his daughter Gianna right by his side. Both father and daughter were warmly embraced by players before, during, and after the game.[256]

The hoodie worn by Bryant was more than a fashion statement. In our interview, Meredith Cash, Sports Reporter for *Business Insider*, explained what he meant to the league. "Kobe was so much more than just an avid WNBA fan. He had a good relationship with WNBA Commissioner Cathy Engelbert and kept up-to-date with happenings in the league. He was invested in the WNBA's growth and the growth of the women's game on the whole, not only for his daughter Gigi but for other up-and-coming stars as well."

Cash continues, "Above all else, though, Kobe provided 'legitimacy to our game,' according to LA Sparks star Chiney Ogwumike. Just by nature of who he was and how his name and likeness was practically synonymous with cool, Kobe's affinity for the W helped give its players credibility and silence its critics."[257]

As one decade came to a close and another began, Nike teamed up with Bryant and challenged themselves to find a way to improve an already high-performing sneaker. Remaining true to the vision of the Protro series, the Nike Zoom Kobe 5 Protro made significant upgrades. Starting with the upper, Nike said they simplified the construction to create a softer feel without sacrificing support and impact protection. The cushion switched from a Phylon midsole to a plush Cushlon midsole. The Zoom Air unit in the heel was removed, while a large-volume Zoom Turbo unit went under the forefoot. The design team tweaked traction by scaling down the outsole's surface area for an improved grip.[258]

On December 26, 2019 the Nike Kobe 5 "Chaos Alternate" colorway was available exclusively to gamers on NBA2K20. If gamers surpassed Bryant's Christmas Day scoring high of 42 points in a MyPLAYER Nation game, they unlocked the chance to get a digital version of the sneakers. Additionally, they would be granted access to purchase a physical version through the Nike SNKRS app.[259] However, it was rumored to have been limited to only 2,200 pairs. On January 3, 2020, the Nike Kobe 5 Protro "Joker" colorway hit shelves for $180.

Of course, it didn't take long for NBA players to lace up the Kobe 5 Protro on the court. More than a decade since Bryant debuted them on Christmas Day, and the sneakers were more popular than ever. To add fuel to the hype fire, Nike planned to release a "Big Stage" colorway that combined the black-and-white OG colorways from 2010.

As a sign of the times, records were being broken. On January 25, LeBron James passed Bryant on the NBA All-Time Scoring List in Bryant's hometown of Philadelphia. At 10:39 p.m. Bryant tweeted, "Continuing to move the game forward @KingJames. Much respect my brother (flexed bicep emoji) #3364." Not long after, he posted a picture of the two from the Mavericks game on December 28, 2018.

The Instagram caption read, "On to #2 @KingJames! Keep growing the game and charting the path to the next (flexed bicep emoji)."[260]

Since 2003, members of the sports media tried everything in their power to pit the two against each other. Even worse, they divided the two loyal fan bases. On that historic night, television talk show hosts tweeted denigrating remarks they ended up deleting hours later. Despite the perceived rivalry, there was nothing but love and admiration between the two legends. From high school to the NBA to the Olympics, all they cared about was each other and pushing the game forward.

*　*　*

The events of January 26, 2020 were not supposed to happen. It made no sense. The lives lost in the helicopter crash were priceless. As the news broke, the whole world cried together. Statements from presidents, athletes, musicians, filmmakers, authors, and people from every walk of life quickly started appearing online. For weeks, people all over the globe mourned the lives lost in the accident. Tributes came in all forms. Buildings lit up, murals were painted, flowers and gifts appeared in front of the Staples Center. Stories of secret acts of kindness by Bryant finally saw the light of day.

Naturally, fans tried to fill the Kobe-and-Gianna-sized holes in their hearts with memorabilia. Every piece of Bryant merchandise available (especially sneakers) flew off the shelves. Nike made the prudent decision to postpone restocking merchandise out of respect to the Bryant family and the other families who lost loved ones. Searching his name on retail websites showed no available goods and redirected fans to a Nike statement titled "In Memory: Kobe Bryant"[261]

The statement read:

> *"Kobe was one of the greatest athletes of his generation and has had an immeasurable impact on the world of sport and the community of basketball. He was a beloved member of the Nike family. We will miss him greatly. Mamba forever."*

Adidas remembered Bryant by posting a black and white photo

of a young Bryant backwards dunking in a pair of KB8 alongside a heartfelt message on their social media platforms.[262] The statement read:

> "The Adidas family's hearts are with the families, friends, and all those affected by today's tragedy. Kobe was a true legend who inspired others beyond the boundaries of the game. He will be greatly missed.
> Mamba forever."

All across the NBA, players and teams honored the lives of Kobe and Gianna. Special sneakers, changed jersey numbers, video tributes, moments of silence, and eight-second backcourt violations followed by 24-second shot clock violations took place in every arena. After postponing a regular season game against the Clippers, the Lakers played for the first time against the Trail Blazers on January 31. Before the game, the Lakers held an emotional tribute to the Bryant family. Usher sang "Amazing Grace," Boys II Men sang the National Anthem. Los Angeles philharmonic cellist Ben Hong set the background music during a stirring video tribute. A teary-eyed LeBron James took the microphone and gave a pitch-perfect speech to the emotional Staples Center crowd. James ended with, "In the words of Kobe Bryant—Mamba out. But in the words of us, not forgotten. Live on, brother."[263] At halftime of the game, Wiz Khalifa and Charlie Puth reunited to perform "See You Again." The game took a backseat to the importance of the night.

On January 28, ESPN *SportsCenter* host Elle Duncan shared her story of when she met Bryant. It was when she was eight-months pregnant and expecting a baby girl. Duncan recounted how excited that made Bryant and how he wished he could have five more girls. Bryant said, "I'm a girl dad!" Shortly after the segment ended, the hashtag #GirlDad started trending on social media. Fathers were posting pictures with their daughters and expressing what it meant to them to have daughters.[264]

At the 2020 NBA All-Star Game held in Chicago, the league honored Kobe and Gianna in several ways. First by renaming the All-Star Game Most Valuable Player Award after Kobe. Second, Team LeBron wore number 2 (Gianna's jersey number) on their jerseys, while Team Giannis wore number 24 (Kobe's jersey number) on their jerseys. Third, the exhibition game format was changed to include an Elam Ending with the target score of 24.[265] Additionally, there were touching musical tributes from Chance the Rapper, Common, Jennifer Hudson, and Maroon 5. It was an incredibly bittersweet weekend for the NBA, which helped heal the fans all over the world who were still hurting after three weeks.

On February 24 (2/24—Gianna and Kobe's numbers), a public memorial was held inside the Staples Center. Athletes, celebrities, and fans filled the stands, wanting one last opportunity to celebrate the lives of Kobe and Gianna. Jimmy Kimmel hosted the event, while Beyonce, Alicia Keys, and Christina Aguilera performed.[266] Nike debuted a nearly two-minute long video tribute titled *Mamba Forever*. Speakers included Michael Jordan, Shaquille O'Neal, Sabrina Ionescu, Diana Taurasi, Geno Auriemma, and Rob Pelinka. To everyone's surprise, Vanessa spoke as well. Despite unimaginable emotional pain and grief, Vanessa summed up her late husband and daughter's lives better than anyone. Her strength gave everyone else the courage to honor Kobe and Gianna by carrying on and chasing their dreams the way the father-and-daughter duo did.

The 2020 WNBA draft took place on April 17. Gianna Bryant, Alyssa Altobelli, and Payton Chester were selected as honorary draft picks. Additionally, WNBA commissioner Cathy Engelbert announced the new Kobe & Gigi Bryant WNBA Advocacy Award, which recognizes "an individual or group who has made significant contributions to the visibility, perception, and advancement of women's and girls' basketball at all levels."[267]

Beginning on August 23, Nike kicked off the first-ever "Mamba Week," which included special programming and launches. Several Kobe signature products were released, and the Nike Foundation donated $1 million to the Mamba and Mambacita Sports Foundation. As part of the celebration, Nike released five pairs of Kobe 5 Protro. Two Undefeated (UNDFTD) collaborations in the "What If" pack that used colorways to reimagine what could have happened if Bryant had not ended up with the Lakers.[268] Additionally, an EYBL PE, and both of the previously postponed "5X Champ" and "Big Stage" colorways dropped in the same week. Both the "5 Rings" and "Bruce Lee" colorways released later that fall. But most importantly, LeBron James and Anthony Davis led the Los Angeles Lakers to a championship on October 11.

Note from the Author

Bryant's legacy is still hard to fathom. He was a larger-than-life character who overshadowed the entertainment capital of the world. His unrelenting self-confidence willed him to places most never dream of. That fearlessness inspired more people than his fadeaway jumper ever could. His philosophy, Mamba Mentality, impacted millions of lives for the better. All over the world right now, there are individuals in every industry who are pushing themselves to become the best at what they do because of Bryant.

Bryant's fingerprints are all over basketball and the sneaker industry. There are hundreds of Bryant's acolytes in the NBA, WNBA, and international leagues who will carry on his memory. It's a massive understatement to say new generations of players will be influenced by Bryant for decades to come.

Long after the human race is gone, Bryant will be inspiring otherworldly beings in the universe. It brings a smile to my face to imagine the year 30,233 and aliens landing on Earth and getting their minds blown by watching archaic footage of Bryant. There is no doubt they would recreate some pairs of the Nike Kobe 9 Elite and lace them halfway up their little green legs and start reenacting moments from his career.

5 . . . 4 . . . 3 . . .

The alien takes the ball to the corner, where she is met by a double team.

2 . . . 1 . . .

She lifts up, releases the ball as time expires, and shouts, "KO-BE!"

Acknowledgements

This book did not get written without the following people taking time out of their busy schedules to help a total stranger.

Chris Chase's years of documenting Kobe's sneakers on WearTesters.com provided the foundation of this book. I relied heavily on his archived work and clear explanations of sophisticated technology. His video for the Kobe 11 EM got me into sneakers, and I've been his fan ever since.

Rudy Garciduenas was a pillar in the Lakers organization for over a quarter century. He was right by Bryant's side from first day as a Laker to the night he became a five-time champion. Garciduenas took time from running his business to answer a litany of questions that spanned over 15 years.

Dr. Tim DiFrancesco worked closely with Bryant during the most physically challenging time in his career. I sincerely appreciate him taking time away from his new business to share personal stories from his time with the Lakers.

Anthony Gilbert knew the Bryant family for decades. He covered Kobe from his high school days to the end of his career. He is incredibly protective of the family, and I am truly indebted to him for his honesty and candor.

Matt Welty is not only an Adidas historian but an encyclopedia for all things sneakers. His writing, podcast, and YouTube show made me dig deeper to provide as much historical context as possible.

Jarrel Harris is an excellent writer who has been around for some significant moments in Kobe's sneaker history. His passion and knowledge about hoops inspires me to work harder. I hope to one day be as good at this craft as he is.

Jeffrey M. Jordan had every right to ignore me when I emailed him tons of questions, but he never did. Despite balancing several important jobs, he always took the time to provide thorough and honest answers.

Meredith Cash has a way of writing that is both thoughtful and rigorous. Every time I read something she publishes, it challenges me to think outside my perspective. Her coverage of women's sports, specifically the WNBA, has taught me so much.

Harrison Faigen took time away from his honeymoon and the Lakers championship run to answer every question I had from his early days as a reporter. His journalism is airtight, and I can't wait to read the book he writes in the future about his time covering the Lakers.

Xinjie is a testament to the global popularity of Bryant. All Kobe fans and sneakerheads must keep up with the amazing curatorial work he is doing in his museum in Beijing.

Special thanks to Enchanted Ink Publishing. Natalia Leigh, Meredith Spears, and Greg Rupel were integral in turning this dream into a reality. I relied upon their expertise every single step of the way. The only thing stronger than their work ethic is their genuine goodness.

Big shoutout to Basketball-Reference. All statistics, box-scores, schedules, results, and rosters in this book came from the best basketball database in the world. Please support the work they are doing on that website.

Many thanks to the following sneaker blogs for their journalism throughout the years:

Complex, Kicks on Fire, Nice Kicks, Sole Collector, Sneaker Bar Detroit, Sneaker Files, and *Sneaker News.*

I'm grateful for all of the Kobe fan accounts on Instagram that constantly unearth moments from Bryant's amazing life: @Countonkobe, @goatout, @iskobebryant, @kb824, @kobe.clips, @kobegram, @kobepost, @mamba24ever, @oneluvkobe24, @thebookofkobe, and @vegaslakersfans, just to name a few.

I am in no way affiliated with the following organizations, but I encourage to you to donate to the Kobe Bryant and Vanessa Bryant Family Foundation (kvbff.org) as well as the Mamba On Three Fund (mambaonthree.org).

Notes and Sources

Chapter 1: Fresh Prince

Endnotes

1. Lazenby, Roland. "Chapter 13: The Rising." *Showboat: The Life of Kobe Bryant*, 144–45. New York, NY: Little, Brown and Company, 2016.
2. Ibid, 161.
3. Ibid, 201.
4. Ibid, 205.
5. Sole Collector. "Flashback Frida: Adidas EQT Top Ten 2010." Sole Collector. Sole Collector, November 3, 2018. https://solecollector.com/news/2009/06/flashback-friday-adidas-eqt-top-ten-2010.
6. Matt Welty, e-mail message to the author. August 18, 2020.
7. Ibid.
8. Schlemmer, Zack. "Kobe Bryant's 20 Year Sneaker Legacy – Part 1: The Adidas Years." Sneaker News, August 8, 2016. https://sneakernews.com/2016/02/18/kobe-bryants-20-year-sneaker-legacy-part-1-the-adidas-years/.
9. My VHS Collection. "ADIDAS Commercial "Feet You Wear" with Kobe Bryant." YouTube video, 00:30. Posted by "My VHS Collection." September 1, 2019. https://www.youtube.com/watch?v=v8u2I8RngOo.
10. Sole Collector. "Flashback Frida: Adidas EQT Top Ten 2010." Sole Collector. Sole Collector, November 3, 2018. https://solecollector.com/news/2009/06/flashback-friday-adidas-eqt-top-ten-2010.
11. "Adidas Crazy 97 (EQT Elevation): Adidas." Sole Collector. Accessed September 12, 2020. https://solecollector.com/sd/00936/adidas/adidas-crazy-97-eqt-elevation.
12. DaniBoxx. "Kobe Bryant Adidas Rookie Commercial." YouTube video, 00:36. Posted by DaniBoxx. March 11, 2007. https://www.youtube.com/watch?v=gEcyhWJkQXI
13. Fromal, Adam. "Kobe Bryant Declined Jesus Shuttlesworth Role Before It Was Given to Ray Allen." Bleacher Report. Bleacher Report, October 3, 2017. https://bleacherreport.com/articles/1814813-kobe-bryant-declined-jesus-shuttlesworth-role-before-it-was-given-to-ray-allen.
14. Boon. "Kobe Bryant's Best-Ever Adidas Signature Sneakers." Sneaker Freaker. Accessed September 13, 2020. https://www.sneakerfreaker.com/features/the-best-of-adidas-era-kobe-bryant.

15	Tesema, Feleg. "10 Of the Best Adidas Torsion Sneakers Out Now." Highsnobiety, October 28, 2019. https://www.highsnobiety.com/p/best-adidas-torsion-sneakers-buy-online/.
16	Piotrekzprod. "Kobe Bryant EVERY Adidas Shoe Commercial (1996-2004) HD." YouTube video, 8:04. Posted by Piotrekzprod. January 11, 2018. https://www.youtube.com/watch?v=flUPpXVYHYU
17	Rudy Garciduenas, e-mail message to the author. August 20, 2020.
18	Folkert Leffring. "1998 Kobe Bryant mixtape - with his sister." YouTube video, 2:16. Posted by Folkert Leffring. May 2, 2013. https://www.youtube.com/watch?v=jEs_TuABWxE&t=1s
19	Anthony Gilbert, e-mail message to the author. August 13, 2020.
20	WearTesters. "adidas Crazy 2 (KB II) Retro." YouTube video, 3:34. Posted by WearTesters. June 14, 2014. https://www.youtube.com/watch?v=hfxtxj6mrRQ
21	Piotrekzprod. "Kobe Bryant EVERY Adidas Shoe Commercial (1996-2004)."
22	Schlemmer. "Kobe Bryant's 20 Year Sneaker Legacy – Part 1: The Adidas Years."
23	Piotrekzprod. "Kobe Bryant EVERY Adidas Shoe Commercial (1996-2004)."
24	Hunter Fairhall Kirkman. "Spalding | Commercial - (1999)." YouTube video, 00:33. Posted by Hunter Fairhall Kirkman.
25	"NBA Courtside 2 Featuring Kobe Bryant N64." NBA Courtside 2 Featuring Kobe Bryant | N64, n.d. http://rarity.club/games/N64/NBA-Courtside-2-Featuring-Kobe-Bryant.
26	Jason. "Kobe Bryant's Adidas Forum 2000 Shoes." What Pros Wear, April 16, 2019. https://www.whatproswear.com/basketball/kobe-bryant/shoes/kobe-bryants-adidas-forum-2000-shoes/.
27	"Lakers Uniforms." LakerStats.com, September 7, 2020. https://www.lakerstats.com/lakers-uniforms/.

Chapter 2: California Love

28	"Adidas Crazy 1 (The Kobe): Adidas." Sole Collector. Accessed September 14, 2020. https://solecollector.com/sd/00889/adidas/adidas-crazy-1-the-kobe.
29	Piotrekzprod. "Kobe Bryant EVERY Adidas Shoe Commercial (1996-2004)."
30	Schlemmer. "Kobe Bryant's 20 Year Sneaker Legacy – Part 1: The Adidas Years."
31	Lazenby, *Showboat*, 361.

32 Analog Indulgence. "Spalding NBA Basketball (2002) Television Commercial - Kobe Bryant – Infusion." YouTube video, 00:30. Posted by Analog Indulgence. July 9, 2020. https://www.youtube.com/watch?v=RBDX5PxCYZM
33 Piotrekzprod. "Kobe Bryant EVERY Adidas Shoe Commercial (1996-2004)."
34 Danforth, Chris. "Adidas Kobe 2: A Look Back at Kobe Bryant's Most Bizarre Sneaker." Highsnobiety, August 27, 2020. https://www.highsnobiety.com/p/adidas-kobe-2-history/.
35 McMenamin, Dave. "LeBron James Looking Forward to Matchup with Kobe Bryant." ESPN. ESPN Internet Ventures, February 9, 2016. https://www.espn.com/nba/story/_/id/14744395/lebron-james-looking-forward-cleveland-cavaliers-wednesday-matchup-kobe-bryant-los-angeles-lakers.
36 Lazenby, *Showboat*, 402.
37 Matt Welty, e-mail message to the author. August 18, 2020.
38 Ibid.
39 "Nike Signs Kobe Bryant To $40 Million Contract." The Wall Street Journal, June 25, 2003. https://www.wsj.com/articles/SB105649507860753000.
40 Mitchell, Alex. "Reliving Kobe Bryant's Rucker Park Game in 2002." amNewYork, January 27, 2020. https://www.amny.com/sports/reliving-kobe-bryants-rucker-park-game-in-2002/.

Chapter 3: Free Agency

41 Stonebrook, Ian. "Kobe Bryant Playing in Air Jordans Complete History & Points." Nice Kicks, March 28, 2020. https://www.nicekicks.com/kobe-playing-in-air-jordans/.
42 Boon. "Looking Back at Kobe Bryant's 2002-2003 Sneaker Free Agency." Sneaker Freaker, June 30, 2019. https://www.sneakerfreaker.com/features/looking-back-at-kobe-bryants-sneaker-free-agency-in-2002-2003?page=2.
43 Rudy Garciduenas, e-mail message to the author. August 20, 2020.
44 Jeffrey Jordan, e-mail message to the author. August 22, 2020.

Chapter 4: The Swoosh

45 Rovell, Darren. ESPN. ESPN Internet Ventures, June 18, 2003. https://www.espn.com/nba/news/2003/0618/1570090.html.

46	Brown, Tim. "Kobe Finds Sole Mate." Los Angeles Times. Los Angeles Times, June 24, 2003. https://www.latimes.com/archives/la-xpm-2003-jun-24-sp-kobe24-story.html.
47	Chase, Chris. "Nike Zoom Huarache 2k4 Performance Review." WearTesters, October 9, 2019. https://weartesters.com/nike-zoom-huarache-2k4-performance-review/.
48	Zack, Schlemmer. "Kobe Bryant's 20 Year Sneaker Legacy - Part 3: The Early Nike Years." Sneaker News, March 24, 2016. https://sneakernews.com/2016/03/24/kobe-bryants-20-year-sneaker-legacy-part-3-the-early-nike-years/.
49	Ibid.
50	Press, Associated. "Kobe Remains with Lakers." ESPN. ESPN Internet Ventures, July 15, 2004. https://www.espn.com/nba/news/story?id=1840336.
51	Gaines, Cork. "Kobe Bryant Created His 'Black Mamba' Alter-Ego as a Way to Get through the Lowest Point of His Career." Business Insider. Business Insider, January 27, 2020. https://www.businessinsider.com/kobe-bryant-black-mamba-nickname-2015-3.
52	Schlemmer. "Kobe Bryant's 20 Year Sneaker Legacy - Part 3: The Early Nike Years."
53	Wollman, Seth. "Nike Air Huarache 2k5 // Throwback Thursday." Nice Kicks, August 9, 2018. https://www.nicekicks.com/nike-air-huarache-2k5-throwback-thursday/.
54	"Nike Free Footwear Platform." Nike News, March 19, 2019. https://news.nike.com/news/what-is-nike-free.
55	Bresnahan, Mike. "Lakers Turn to Hire Power." Los Angeles Times. Los Angeles Times, June 15, 2005. https://www.latimes.com/archives/la-xpm-2005-jun-15-sp-jackson15-story.html.
56	Astramskas, David. "The NBA Dress Code of 2005: Why It Was Created & How Players Reacted To It." Ballislife.com, October 17, 2018. https://ballislife.com/remembering-when-the-nba-created-a-dress-code-in-2005-was-it-racist/.
57	Schlemmer. "Kobe Bryant's 20 Year Sneaker Legacy - Part 3: The Early Nike Years."
58	Sager, Mike. "Kobe Bryant Doesn't Want Your Love." Esquire, August 21, 2020. https://www.esquire.com/sports/a3588/kobebryant1107/.
59	"Kobe Bryant Logo Meaning." Paul, Basketball, and Josh, November 6, 2012. "Kobe Bryant Logo Meaning." Paul, Basketball, and Josh, November 6, 2012. https://pbandjbasketball.blogspot.com/2012/11/kobe-bryant-logo-meaning.html.
60	Wollman. "Nike Air Huarache 2k5 // Throwback Thursday."

Chapter 5: Black Mamba

61. Chase, Chris. "Nike Kobe 1 Protro Performance Review." WearTesters, October 9, 2019. https://weartesters.com/nike-kobe-1-protro-performance-review/.
62. Schlemmer, Zack. "Nike Air Max Uptempo History." Sneaker News, December 14, 2016. https://sneakernews.com/2016/12/14/nike-air-max-uptempo-history/.
63. Rudy Garciduenas, e-mail message to the author. August 20, 2020.
64. Jsantos1724. "The 81 Point Game – January 22, 2006." Kobe24-8.com, January 22, 2014. https://kb824.wordpress.com/2014/01/22/the-81-point-game-january-22-2006/.
65. Piotrekzprod. "Kobe Bryant EVERY Nike Shoe Commercial (2005-2017) HD." YouTube video, 12:50. Posted by Piotrekzprod. September 3, 2017. https://www.youtube.com/watch?v=fYBCkz06vmQ&t
66. Theassistant32. "Kobe Game-Tying + Game Winning Shot vs Suns 06 Play-Offs HD." YouTube video, 6:32. Posted by, Theassistant32. June 1, 2008. https://www.youtube.com/watch?v=ACZnF87Iy84
67. Holmes, Baxter. "Kobe Bryant Is Finally Ready to Say Goodbye to the NBA." ESPN. ESPN Internet Ventures, December 17, 2017. https://www.espn.com/nba/story/_/id/21785439/how-kobe-bryant-legacy-forced-los-angeles-lakers-retire-two-numbers-nba.
68. Schlemmer. "Kobe Bryant's 20 Year Sneaker Legacy - Part 3: The Early Nike Years."
69. Schwollo. "Retro Performance Review: Nike Zoom Kobe II." schwollo.com, March 30, 2015. https://schwollo.com/2015/04/01/retro-review-nike-zoom-kobe-ii/.
70. Piotrekzprod. "Kobe Bryant EVERY Nike Shoe Commercial (2005-2017) HD."
71. "Nike Air Zoom Kobe II 2 2007 History." SneakerFiles. Accessed September 14, 2020. https://www.sneakerfiles.com/nike/nike-basketball/nike-air-zoom-kobe-ii-2/.
72. Lazenby, *Showboat*, 496.
73. "An Explanation of Every Jersey Number Worn by Kobe Bryant." Pro Hoops Journal, September 1, 2010. http://prohoopsjournal.com/2010/09/kobe-bryant-by-the-numbers/.
74. "Kobe Bryant SUPERNATURAL Asian Tour September 2007 by Nike." Hibachibaby.wordpress.com, August 29, 2007. https://hibachibaby.wordpress.com/2007/08/24/kobe-bryant-supernatural-asian-tour-september-2007-by-nike/.
75. Schlemmer. "Kobe Bryant's 20 Year Sneaker Legacy - Part 3: The Early Nike Years."

76. Betschart, Brian. "Nike Zoom 2K4 Huarache Kobe Lasers Black/Purple Release in USA." SneakerFiles, November 14, 2017. https://www.sneakerfiles.com/nike-zoom-2k4-huarache-kobe-lasers-black-purple-release-in-usa/.
77. Schlemmer. "Kobe Bryant's 20 Year Sneaker Legacy - Part 3: The Early Nike Years."
78. Spark. "Review: Nike Zoom Kobe III." Kicksologists.com, April 16, 2010. https://www.kicksologists.com/2010/03/15/nike-zoom-kobe-iii/.
79. Schwollo. "Retro Review: Nike Zoom Kobe III." schwollo.com, May 16, 2015. https://schwollo.com/2015/05/18/retro-review-nike-zoom-kobe-iii/.
80. KixandtheCity.com "KixandtheCity.com: Kobe Bryant on the Nike Zoom Kobe III." YouTube video, 4:24. Posted by KixandtheCity.com January 3, 2008. https://www.youtube.com/watch?v=rJA1pFlh1pY
81. "Lakers' Throwback Jerseys Feature Short Shorts Worn by Magic." ESPN. ESPN Internet Ventures, December 31, 2007. https://www.espn.com/nba/news/story?id=3174399.
82. Piotrekzprod. "Kobe Bryant EVERY Nike Shoe Commercial (2005-2017) ᴴᴰ."
83. "Kobe Bryant: Shoe History: Sneaker Pics and Commercials." Kicksologists.com, n.d. https://www.kicksologists.com/kobe-bryant-sneakers/.
84. Betschart, Brian. "Nike Zoom Kobe III (3) Lakers China Edition." SneakerFiles, November 27, 2015. https://www.sneakerfiles.com/nike-zoom-kobe-iii-3-lakers-china-edition/.
85. Rudy Garciduenas, e-mail message to the author. August 20, 2020.
86. Sole Collector. "Nike Hyperdunk Performance Review." Sole Collector, June 1, 2018. https://solecollector.com/news/2009/08/nike-hyperdunk-performance-review.
87. Lund, Spencer. "10 Years Later: Kobe Jumping an Aston Martin Made the Nike Hyperdunk a Viral Sneaker." Complex. Complex, June 1, 2018. https://www.complex.com/sneakers/2018/04/10-years-later-kobe-bryant-jumping-an-aston-martin-made-the-nike-hyperdunk-a-viral-sneaker.
88. Herbert, James. "Kobe Hate-Listened to 'Don't Stop Believin'' for 2 Years after Celtics Loss." CBSSports.com, April 6, 2017. https://www.cbssports.com/nba/news/kobe-hate-listened-to-dont-stop-believin-for-2-years-after-celtics-loss/.
89. Jones, Riley. "TBT: Kobe Bryant Pulls Up in a DeLorean to Release the 'Marty McFly' Nike Hyperdunks." Complex. Complex, April 20, 2020. https://www.complex.com/sneakers/2016/04/tbt-kobe-bryant-delorean-nike-hyperdunk-mcfly.

Chapter 6: Ringsssss

90   Richard, Brandon. "Kobe Bryant, the Redeem Team, and How the Hyperdunk Changed Nike Basketball." Sole Collector. Sole Collector, June 1, 2018. https://solecollector.com/news/2015/08/how-the-hyperdunk-changed-nike-basketball.

91   Chase, Chris. "Nike Kobe 4 Protro Performance Review." WearTesters, October 9, 2019. https://weartesters.com/nike-kobe-4-protro-performance-review/.

92   Chris Chase, e-mail message to the author. August 11, 2020.

93   Anthony Gilbert, e-mail message to the author. August 13, 2020.

94   Sneakernews. "NBA Feet - Christmas Day 2008." Sneaker News, June 23, 2009. https://sneakernews.com/2008/12/26/nba-feet-christmas-day-2008/.

95   "Nike ID Zoom Kobe IV Cut ID - Christmas." Sneaker News, June 26, 2009. https://sneakernews.com/2008/12/11/nike-zoom-kobe-iv-nike-id/.

96   Piotrekzprod. "Kobe Bryant EVERY Nike Shoe Commercial (2005-2017) [HD]."

97   "Mistakes Were Made: The Nike Zoom Kobe 4 Draft Day Blunder." Kicks On Fire, December 2, 2015. https://www.kicksonfire.com/mistakes-were-made-nike-zoom-kobe-4-draft-day/.

98   "Kobe Bryant: Shoe History: Sneaker Pics and Commercials." Kicksologists.com, n.d.

99   Yeboah, Kofie. "Remember When Nike's Kobe and LeBron Puppets Celebrated Christmas with a Holiday Rap Battle?" SBNation.com. SBNation.com, December 22, 2017. https://www.sbnation.com/2017/12/22/16682834/nba-christmas-commercial-kobe-lebron-puppets-nike.

100   "CPS Students Design Shoes for Kobe Bryant: ABC7 Chicago." ABC7 Chicago, March 24, 2009. https://abc7chicago.com/archive/6720357/.

101   Betschart, Brian. "Nike Zoom Kobe IV (4) - Black Mamba." SneakerFiles, March 21, 2009. https://www.sneakerfiles.com/nike-zoom-kobe-iv-4-black-mamba/.

102   "Kobe Bryant Recalls The Time Lil Wayne Made A Song About Him." Genius, January 21, 2019. https://genius.com/a/kobe-bryant-recalls-the-time-lil-wayne-made-a-song-about-him.

103   Betschart, Brian. "Nike Zoom Kobe IV (4) MVP." SneakerFiles, March 13, 2014. https://www.sneakerfiles.com/nike-zoom-kobe-iv-4-mvp/.

104   Mozartofbasketball. "Conan O'Brien show 2009 Kobe Bryant." YouTube video, 10:15. Posted by Mozartofbasketball. January 27, 2020. https://www.youtube.com/watch?v=leOYxst8ago

105   Mina, Rosanna. "Kobe Bryant Caps off Manila Leg of Asia Tour." ABS. ABS-CBN News, July 23, 2009. https://news.abs-cbn.com/sports/07/21/09/kobe-bryant-caps-manila-leg-asia-tour.

106   Kr, Aaron. "Nike Dream Season - Kobe Bryant - Fall/Winter '09." Sneaker News, April 10, 2009. https://sneakernews.com/2009/04/10/nike-dream-season-kobe-bryant-fallwinter-09/.

107   "Nike Zoom Kobe IV Gradient – Home vs Away." Kicks on Fire, November 10, 2009. https://www.kicksonfire.com/nike-zoom-kobe-iv-gradient-home-vs-away/.

108   Ruano, Luis. "Nike Zoom Kobe IV '4 Rings' Quickstrike." HYPEBEAST, September 29, 2009. https://hypebeast.com/2009/9/nike-zoom-kobe-iv-4-rings-quickstrike.

109   WearTesters. "Nike Zoom Kobe V 5 Performance Review." YouTube video, 9:59. Posted by WearTesters. June 17, 2010. https://www.youtube.com/watch?v=FBzS6zDp1Zc&t=523s

110   Torres, Luis. "The Significance of the Nike Zoom Kobe 5 a Decade Later." Nice Kicks, August 23, 2020. https://www.nicekicks.com/kobe-bryant-nike-zoom-kobe-5-history/.

111   Kr, Aaron. "Nike Zoom Kobe V ID Presentation @ The Montalban Theatre." Sneaker News, December 9, 2009. https://sneakernews.com/2009/12/09/nike-zoom-kobe-v-id-presentation-the-montalban-theatre/.

112   "Kobe Bryant: Shoe History: Sneaker Pics and Commercials." Kicksologists.com, n.d.

113   Kan, Eugene. "Bruce Lee x Nike Zoom Kobe V & Promotional Posters." HYPEBEAST, February 3, 2010. https://hypebeast.com/2010/2/bruce-lee-nike-zoom-kobe-promotional-posters.

114   Bkrw. "Nike Kobe "ALL TOGETHER NOW" video." YouTube video, 1:11. Posted by Bkrw. June 4, 2010. https://www.youtube.com/watch?v=huHmHshx9g0

115   Kim, John. "Nike Zoom Kobe V (5) - Big Stage Graphic - Closer Look." Sneaker News, July 29, 2010. https://sneakernews.com/2010/07/29/nike-zoom-kobe-v-5-big-stage-graphic-closer-look/.

116   Kim, John. "Nike Zoom Kobe V (5) - Big Stage: Release Info." Sneaker News, August 3, 2010. https://sneakernews.com/2010/08/03/nike-zoom-kobe-v-5-big-stage-release-info/amp/.

Chapter 7: Lows

117   Press, Associated. "Bryant Visits Soweto, Attends U.S. Game." ESPN. ESPN Internet Ventures, June 27, 2010. https://www.espn.com/los-angeles/story/_/id/5334728/ce/us/world-cup-draws-kobe-bryant-south-africa.

118	"London Called, but Lakers Don't Figure to Be Back Any Time Soon." ESPN. ESPN Internet Ventures, October 5, 2010. https://www.espn.com/blog/los-angeles/lakers/post/_/id/10858/london-called-but-lakers-dont-figure-to-be-back-any-time-soon.
119	Kim, John. "Nike Zoom Kobe VI (6) - Bottom Sole Design." Sneaker News, August 30, 2010. https://sneakernews.com/2010/08/30/nike-zoom-kobe-vi-6-bottom-sole-design/.
120	"Nike Launches Zoom Kobe VI." Nike News, December 7, 2010. https://news.nike.com/news/nike-launches-zoom-kobe-vi.
121	Hope, Aaron. "Nike Zoom Kobe VI - Available on Nike ID." Sneaker News, December 21, 2010. https://sneakernews.com/2010/12/21/nike-zoom-kobe-vi-available-on-nike-id/.
122	Anthony Gilbert, e-mail message to the author. August 13, 2020.
123	Piotrekzprod. "Kobe Bryant EVERY Nike Shoe Commercial (2005-2017) HD."
124	"Kobe Bryant: Shoe History: Sneaker Pics and Commercials." Kicksologists.com, n.d.
125	Richard, Brandon. "News: New York's Rice High School Closing Next Month." Sole Collector. Sole Collector, June 1, 2018. https://solecollector.com/news/2011/05/news-new-york-s-rice-high-school-closing-next-month.
126	Jarrel Harris, e-mail message to the author. August 17, 2020.
127	Rudy Garciduenas, e-mail message to the author. August 20, 2020.
128	Ibid.
129	"NBA Star Kobe Kicks off Asia Tour in Philippines." sina_com, July 13, 2011. http://english.sina.com/sports/p/2011/0713/380849.html.
130	Kamenetzky, Andy. "How Kobe Ended up at Drew League." ESPN. ESPN Internet Ventures, August 18, 2011. https://www.espn.com/blog/los-angeles/lakers/post/_/id/21770/how-kobe-ended-up-at-drew-league.
131	Foster, D.J. "Chris Paul 'Trade That Wasn't' Timeline." ESPN. ESPN Internet Ventures, December 10, 2011. https://www.espn.com/nba/story/_/page/CP3timeline-111210/breaking-chris-paul-trade-timeline.
132	Kim, John. "Nike Zoom Kobe VII 'Attack Fast' & 'Attack Strong' - Tech Info." Sneaker News, December 7, 2011. https://sneakernews.com/2011/12/07/nike-zoom-kobe-vii-attack-fast-attack-strong-tech-info/.
133	"Introducing the Nike Kobe VII System Supreme." Nike News, December 7, 2011. https://news.nike.com/news/nike-launches-the-nike-zoom-kobe-vii-supreme.
134	Richard, Brandon. "Nike Basketball's Christmas Pack Featured in NBA2K12." Sole Collector. Sole Collector, October 20, 2016. https://solecollector.com/news/2011/12/nike-basketball-s-christmas-pack-featured-in-nba2k12.
135	"Nike Launches 'KobeSystem: Success for the Successful' Campaign." Nike News, January 12, 2012. https://news.nike.com/news/kobesystem-launch.

136   "Kobe Bryant: Shoe History: Sneaker Pics and Commercials." Kicksologists.com, n.d.
137   Sole Collector. "Nike Zoom Kobe 7 Gold Medal: Nike." Sole Collector, February 11, 2016. https://solecollector.com/sd/05423/nike/nike-zoom-kobe-vii-white-metallic-gold-obsidian-true-red.
138   "Nike Hosts Kobe Bryant's Seventh China Tour." Nike News, August 19, 2012. https://news.nike.com/news/nike-hosts-kobe-bryants-seventh-china-tour.
139   @Lakers "Equipment man Carlos Maples estimates that he's got about 150 pairs of shoes waiting for Kobe. Here's some." Instagram, September 27, 2012. https://www.instagram.com/p/QGBuGfLO8q/?hl=en
140   Tim DiFrancesco, phone interview with the author. July 31, 2020.
141   "Nike Unveils the KOBE 8 SYSTEM." Nike News, November 29, 2012. https://news.nike.com/news/nike-unveils-the-kobe-8-system."
142   Ibid.
143   Piotrekzprod. "Kobe Bryant EVERY Nike Shoe Commercial (2005-2017) [HD]."
144   @KobeBryant "The antisocial has become social #mambatweets." Twitter, January 4, 2013. https://twitter.com/kobebryant/status/287245259572903937
145   Sole Collector. "Nike Kobe 8+ - Area 72." Sole Collector, October 20, 2016. https://solecollector.com/news/2013/02/nike-kobe-8-area-72.
146   "Kobe Bryant: Shoe History: Sneaker Pics and Commercials." Kicksologists.com, n.d.
147   Torres, Nick. "Throwback Thursday: Kobe Bryant's 'Amnesty THAT' Game." Lakers Nation, February 23, 2017. https://lakersnation.com/throwback-thursday-kobe-bryants-amnesty-that-game/2017/02/23/.
148   Dwyer, Kelly. "Kobe Bryant Goes on a Facebook Rant, Vowing to Return While Still Casting Doubts about Rehab." Yahoo! Sports. Yahoo!, April 13, 2013. https://sports.yahoo.com/kobe-bryant-goes-facebook-vent-vowing-return-while-151947306--nba.html?y20=1.
149   @KobeBryant "YES! Dominate the boot. Dominate tendons. Dominate the cast. Dominate rehab. Dominate dominating demure dominants domination. Wtf u ask?!? "Your Welcome" #dominatehashtags." Instagram, April 17, 2013. https://www.instagram.com/p/YMrTyARNo8/
150   @KobeBryant "Walking in my "medical mamba" shoes made by Nike in 2 weeks with extra support for the Achilles #alterG #bootoff!" Instagram, May 30, 2013. https://www.instagram.com/p/Z9RKR3xNo9/

Chapter 8: Highs

151   Kim, John. "'Graffiti' Nike Kobe 8 Mid." Sneaker News, August 6, 2013. https://sneakernews.com/2013/07/12/kobe-bryant-in-nike-kobe-8-mid-graffiti-pe/.

152 Tim DiFrancesco, phone interview with the author. July 31, 2020.
153 Chris Chase, e-mail message to the author. August 11, 2020.
154 Xinjie, phone interview with the author. August 16, 2020.
155 Dubasik, Zac. "The Nike Kobe Prelude Pack." Sole Collector, October 20, 2016. https://solecollector.com/news/2013/12/the-nike-kobe-prelude-pack.
156 Golliver, Ben. "Lakers Shut down Kobe Bryant for Rest of Season with Knee Injury." Sports Illustrated, March 12, 2014. https://www.si.com/nba/2014/03/12/kobe-bryant-out-rest-of-season-knee-injury-update.
157 "Nike Redefines Basketball Footwear with the KOBE 9 Elite Featuring Nike Flyknit." Nike News, December 4, 2013. https://news.nike.com/news/kobe9.
158 "Decoding the KOBE 9 Elite Masterpiece." Nike News, February 6, 2014. https://news.nike.com/news/decoding-the-kobe-9-masterpiece.
159 Piotrekzprod. "Kobe Bryant EVERY Nike Shoe Commercial (2005-2017) HD."
160 "Kobe Bryant: Shoe History: Sneaker Pics and Commercials." Kicksologists.com, n.d.
161 "The First of Its Kind: KOBE 9 Elite Low HTM." Nike News, April 8, 2014. https://news.nike.com/news/the-first-of-its-kind-kobe-9-elite-low-htm.
162 Chase, Chris. "Nike Kobe 9 EM Performance Review." WearTesters, August 25, 2020. https://weartesters.com/nike-kobe-9-em-performance-review/.
163 "Kobe Bryant: Shoe History: Sneaker Pics and Commercials." Kicksologists.com, n.d.
164 Sole Collector. "Nike Kobe 9 Elite Low ID Black/Multi-Color: Nike." Sole Collector, February 11, 2016. https://solecollector.com/sd/04387/nike/nike-kobe-9-elite-low-id-black-multi-color.
165 Kim, John. "Kobe Bryant Helps Nike Celebrate The World Cup in Rio." Sneaker News, June 17, 2014. https://sneakernews.com/2014/06/17/kobe-bryant-helps-nike-celebrate-world-cup-rio/.
166 Medina, Mark. "Photo Gallery of Kobe Bryant's Basketball Camp at UC Santa Barbara." Inside the Lakers. Inside the Lakers, July 17, 2014. http://www.insidesocal.com/lakers/2014/07/10/photo-gallery-of-kobe-bryants-basketball-camp-at-uc-santa-barbara/.
167 "Kobe Bryant -- Speaks at Trayvon Martin Event ... I Have 'Responsibility' to Help His Family." TMZ, May 13, 2019. https://www.tmz.com/2014/07/20/kobe-bryant-trayvon-martin-event-responsibility/.
168 "Kobe Bryant Inspires Kids in Greater China to Rise." Nike News, August 7, 2014. https://news.nike.com/news/kobe-bryant-inspires-kids-in-greater-china-to-rise.

169. Schwartz, Nick. "Kobe Bryant Calls ESPN's Experts 'a Bunch of Idiots' for Ranking Him 40th." USA Today. Gannett Satellite Information Network, October 18, 2014. https://ftw.usatoday.com/2014/10/kobe-bryant-espn-idiots-nba-rank.
170. Schlemmer, Zack. "Kobe Bryant Sneaker History Part 5: Nike Flyknit and NBA Farewell." Sneaker News, April 7, 2016. https://sneakernews.com/2016/04/07/kobe-bryants-20-year-sneaker-legacy-part-5-flyknit-farewell/.
171. Ibid.
172. Chase, Chris. "Nike Kobe X (10) Elite Performance Review." WearTesters, October 9, 2019. https://weartesters.com/nike-kobe-x-10-elite-performance-review/.
173. "Kobe Bryant: Shoe History: Sneaker Pics and Commercials." Kicksologists.com, n.d.
174. Winters, Serena. "Kobe Bryant Q&A: The Nike Kobe X Blackout Experience." Lakers Nation, February 22, 2015. https://lakersnation.com/kobe-bryant-qa-the-nike-kobe-x-blackout-experience/2015/02/22/.
175. Briguglio, Mario. "Nike Kobe 10 Elite." Sneaker Bar Detroit, July 4, 2015. https://sneakerbardetroit.com/nike-kobe-10-elite/.
176. "Kobe Bryant: Shoe History: Sneaker Pics and Commercials." Kicksologists.com, n.d.
177. "Multicolor Will Soon Be Available On NIKEiD For The Nike Kobe 10 Elite Low." Kicks on Fire, October 17, 2015. https://www.kicksonfire.com/multicolor-will-soon-be-available-on-nikeid-for-the-nike-kobe-10-elite-low/.
178. Piotrekzprod. "Kobe Bryant EVERY Nike Shoe Commercial (2005-2017) [HD]."
179. "Kobe Bryant Celebrates 10th Asian Summer Tour with Nike." Nike News, August 2, 2015. https://news.nike.com/news/kobe-bryant-china-tour.
180. Briguglio, Mario. "Nike Kobe Venomenon 5 Taipei PE." Sneaker Bar Detroit, May 17, 2017. https://sneakerbardetroit.com/nike-kobe-venomenon-5-taipei-pe/.

Chapter 9: Arrivederci

181. @KobeBryant "First day back on the court shooting! Bout damn time!! #shoulderrecovery #20[th]season @drinkbodyarmor #lakers." Instagram, August 22, 2015. https://www.instagram.com/p/6sy853RNrJ/?hl=en
182. Boudway, Ira. "Kobe Bryant Wants to Sell You a Sports Drink With Bodyarmor." Bloomberg.com. Bloomberg, November 12, 2018. https://www.bloomberg.com/news/features/2018-11-12/kobe-bryant-wants-to-sell-you-a-sports-drink-with-bodyarmor.

183	Adams, Micah. "Kobe Bryant Ranked 93rd in #NBArank Countdown." ESPN. ESPN Internet Ventures, October 7, 2015. https://www.espn.com/blog/statsinfo/post/_/id/110204/kobe-bryant-ranked-93rd-in-nbarank-countdown.
184	"Fall Forecast: Projected NBA Standings." ESPN. ESPN Internet Ventures, October 27, 2015. https://www.espn.com/nba/story/_/id/13980821/projected-standings-2015-16.
185	The Fumble. "Lou Williams Shares Hilarious Story About Kobe Bryant Taking Away Everyone's Kobe Sneakers." YouTube video, 2:38. Posted by The Fumble. January 28, 2020. https://www.youtube.com/watch?v=byxXmD0lg7s
186	Mandell, Nina. "The Lakers Gave Every Fan at Sunday Night's Game a Signed Copy of Kobe's Letter." USA Today. Gannett Satellite Information Network, November 30, 2015. https://ftw.usatoday.com/2015/11/the-lakers-gave-every-fan-at-sunday-nights-game-a-signed-copy-of-kobes-letter.
187	"Remembering Kobe Bryant's Final Game in Philadelphia." NBC10 Philadelphia. NBC 10 Philadelphia, January 26, 2020. https://www.nbcphiladelphia.com/news/sports/sixers/remembering-kobe-bryants-final-game-in-philadelphia/2280102/.
188	Daniels, Tim. "Kobe Bryant Requests Not to Have Gift, Retirement Ceremonies from NBA Teams." Bleacher Report, September 14, 2017. https://bleacherreport.com/articles/2595869-kobe-bryant-requests-not-to-have-gift-retirement-ceremonies-from-nba-teams.
189	Tim DiFrancesco, phone interview with the author. July 31, 2020.
190	"Innovation Mastered: Introducing the KOBE 11." Nike News, December 14, 2015. https://news.nike.com/news/kobe-11.
191	Briguglio, Mario. "NIKEiD Kobe 11." Sneaker Bar Detroit, May 17, 2017. https://sneakerbardetroit.com/nike-id-kobe-11/.
192	"Kobe Bryant: Shoe History: Sneaker Pics and Commercials." Kicksologists.com, n.d.
193	Newport, Kyle. "Kobe Bryant Signs Game-Worn Shoes for LeBron James After Final Game in Cleveland." Bleacher Report, October 3, 2017. https://bleacherreport.com/articles/2615824-kobe-signs-game-worn-shoes-for-lebron.
194	Holmes, Baxter. "NBA Players Turn into Fans in Hunt for Kobe's Autographed Shoes." ESPN. ESPN Internet Ventures, March 29, 2016. https://www.espn.com/nba/story/_/id/15086829/nba-players-turn-fans-seeking-kobe-bryant-autographed-shoes.
195	"Jordan Brand Pays Tribute to Kobe Bryant." Nike News, February 12, 2016. https://news.nike.com/news/jordan-kobe-bryant.
196	Jeffrey Jordan, e-mail message to the author. August 22, 2020.
197	Briguglio, Mario. "Nike Kobe 11 All Star Release Date." Sneaker Bar Detroit, May 17, 2017. https://sneakerbardetroit.com/nike-kobe-11-all-star-release-date/.

198. "Nike Kobe 'Fade To Black' - Release Details: SneakerNews.com ." Sneaker News. Accessed September 15, 2020. https://sneakernews.com/tag/nike-kobe-fade-to-black/.
199. Chase, Chris. "Nike Kobe 11 EM Performance Review." WearTesters, October 9, 2019. https://weartesters.com/nike-kobe-11-em-performance-review/.
200. "Kobe Bryant: Shoe History: Sneaker Pics and Commercials." Kicksologists.com, n.d.
201. Piotrekzprod. "Kobe Bryant EVERY Nike Shoe Commercial (2005-2017) HD."
202. Martinez, Juan. "Nike Celebrates Kobe Bryant With A Countdown To Mamba Day." Kicks on Fire, April 7, 2016. https://www.kicksonfire.com/nike-kobe-bryant-countdown-mamba-day/.
203. "Nike Kobe 11 'Mamba Day' ID Release Date." Nike. Accessed September 15, 2020. https://www.nike.com/launch/t/kobe-11-mamba-day-id.
204. Richard, Brandon. "The 50 Best 'Mamba Day' NIKEiD Kobe 11 Designs." Sole Collector, June 1, 2018. https://solecollector.com/news/2016/06/nike-kobe-11-id-mamba-day-designs/.
205. "Celebrities at Kobe's Last Lakers Game." Los Angeles Times. Los Angeles Times, April 14, 2016. https://www.latimes.com/entertainment/gossip/la-et-mg-celebrities-kobe-bryant-last-lakers-game-20160414-htmlstory.html.
206. Uninterrupted. "Nick Young reminisces about Kobe Bryant | Certified Buckets." YouTube video, 6:27. Posted by Uninterrupted. February 7, 2020. https://www.youtube.com/watch?v=7cWG74OqA7U

Chapter 10: Rebirth

207. "Kobe Bryant Visits Europe to Inspire the Next Generation." *Nike News*, 21 July 2016, news.nike.com/news/kobe-bryant-europe-tour.
208. Tsuji, Alysha. "Kobe Looked Extremely Peaceful While Meditating Outdoors in Taiwan." *USA Today*, Gannett Satellite Information Network, 29 June 2016, ftw.usatoday.com/2016/06/kobe-bryant-meditate-taiwan-photos-manila-beijing.
209. @KobeBryant "Beyond blessed and excited to share that we are expecting our third baby girl!!! #Blessed #BabyMamba #Thankful". Instagram, July 12, 2016. https://www.instagram.com/p/BHyOgV8hix7/?hl=en

210 "CNBC Exclusive: CNBC Transcript: NBA Champion Kobe Bryant and Bryant Stibel General Partner Jeff Stibel Speak with CNBC's 'Squawk on the Street' Today." *CNBC*, CNBC, 22 Aug. 2016, www.cnbc.com/2016/08/22/cnbc-exclusive-cnbc-transcript-nba-champion-kobe-bryant-and-bryant-stibel-general-partner-jeff-stibel-speak-with-cnbcs-squawk-on-the-street-today.html.

211 Neuharth-Keusch, AJ. "City of Los Angeles Declares August 24 'Kobe Bryant Day'." *USA Today*, Gannett Satellite Information Network, 23 Aug. 2016, www.usatoday.com/story/sports/nba/2016/08/23/los-angeles-kobe-bryant-day-august-24/89209846/.

212 Wiedey, Bryan. "NBA 2K17 Gets Early Release Date, Will Be Available Sept. 16." *Sporting News*, 2K Sports, 2 June 2016, www.sportingnews.com/us/nba/news/nba-2k17-to-release-september-16-early-2k-sports-paul-george-kobe-bryant/1ctlnp5fysc9j14bzh4mswaqey.

213 "Nike Kobe AD Reveal: Paying Our Last Respects To The Black Mamba (Kinda…)." *Kicks on Fire*, 1 Nov. 2016, www.kicksonfire.com/nike-kobe-ad-launch-event-recap/.

214 "Introducing the Kobe A.D." *Nike News*, 1 Nov. 2016, news.nike.com/news/kobe-a-d.

215 "Kobe Bryant: Shoe History: Sneaker Pics and Commercials." Kicksologists.com, n.d.

216 "ESPN Teams Up with Kobe Bryant to Present New Content Initiative, 'Canvas'." *SHADOW&ACT*, 20 Apr. 2017, shadowandact.com/espn-teams-up-with-kobe-bryant-to-present-new-content-initiative-canvas.

217 Johnson, Patrick. "Nike Kobe AD Compton Inspired By DeMar DeRozan." *Sneaker News*, 5 Apr. 2017, sneakernews.com/2017/04/05/nike-kobe-ad-compton-release-date-info/.

218 Jones, Riley. "Boston Celtics Star Isaiah Thomas Uses His Sneakers to Honor Late Sister." *Footwear News*, 11 Aug. 2018, footwearnews.com/2017/focus/athletic-outdoor/isaiah-thomas-nike-kobe-sneakers-honor-sister-chyna-boston-celtics-nba-playoffs-339181/.

219 Jarrel Harris, e-mail message to the author. August 17, 2020.

220 Harrison Faigen, e-mail message to the author. August 13, 2020.

221 "The KOBE A.D. NXT Unhinges Tradition." *Nike News*, 29 Mar. 2017, news.nike.com/news/the-kobe-a-d-nxt.

222 Chase, Chris. "Nike Kobe A.D. NXT Performance Review." *WearTesters*, 9 Oct. 2019, weartesters.com/nike-kobe-d-nxt-performance-review/.

223 "Kobe Bryant: Shoe History: Sneaker Pics and Commercials." Kicksologists.com, n.d.

224 "Kobe Bryant vs. Michael Jordan: Who Is Winning the NBA Shoe Game?" *Versus Reviews*, 31 Jan. 2020, versusreviews.com/kobe-bryant-vs-michael-jordan-winning-nba-shoe-game/.

225 "Kobe Bryant Applies Color Psychology to the All-New KOBE A.D." *Nike News*, 14 Aug. 2017, news.nike.com/news/kobe-bryant-kobe-a-d.

226 "Nike Kobe AD Mid Release Date." *Sneaker News*, 15 Aug. 2017, sneakernews.com/2017/08/14/nike-kobe-ad-mid/.
227 Ward-Henninger Aug 24, Colin. "Kobe Bryant Issues Twitter Challenges to Various Athletes ... and Kendrick Lamar?" *CBSSports.com*, 24 Aug. 2017, www.cbssports.com/nba/news/kobe-bryant-issues-twitter-challenges-to-various-athletes-and-kendrick-lamar/.
228 "Kobe Bryant Challenges Giannis Antetokounmpo to Win Kia NBA MVP." *NBA.com*, 27 Aug. 2017, www.nba.com/article/2017/08/27/kobe-bryant-challenges-giannis-antetokounmpo-win-mvp.
229 Gabay, Jalique. "You Can Now Customize the Latest Nike Kobe AD on NIKEiD." *WearTesters*, 9 Oct. 2017, weartesters.com/can-now-customize-latest-nike-kobe-ad-nikeid/.
230 "Kobe Bryant: Shoe History: Sneaker Pics and Commercials." Kicksologists.com, n.d.
231 DeStefano, Mike. "DeMar DeRozan's Kobe A.D. Mid PE Is Coming Soon." *Sole Collector*, Sole Collector, 1 June 2018, solecollector.com/news/2018/05/nike-kobe-ad-mid-demar-derozan-pe-aq2722-900-release-date.
232 Ramirez, Joey. "Lakers Retire Kobe Bryant's Jersey Numbers." *Los Angeles Lakers*, NBA.com/Lakers, 19 Dec. 2017, www.nba.com/lakers/news/171218-kobe-bryant-jersey-retirement.
233 DeStefano, Mike. "Nike Turned LeBron James and Kobe Bryant Into Puppets Again." *Sole Collector*, 19 Dec. 2017, solecollector.com/news/2017/12/nike-brings-back-mvpuppets-commercials-for-kobe-bryant-jersey-retirement.
234 Ota, Kevin. "Exclusively on ESPN+: Detail, From Kobe Bryant's Granity Studios and ESPN, Returning and Expanding to Additional Sports." *ESPN Press Room U.S.*, 17 Oct. 2018, espnpressroom.com/us/press-releases/2018/10/exclusively-on-espn-detail-from-kobe-bryants-granity-studios-and-espn-returning-and-expanding-to-additional-sports/.
235 Polacek, Scott. "Kobe Bryant's 'Dear Basketball' Wins Oscar Award for Best Animated Short Film." *Bleacher Report*, Bleacher Report, 5 Mar. 2018, bleacherreport.com/articles/2762650-kobe-bryants-dear-basketball-wins-oscar-award-for-best-animated-short-film.
236 Schwartz, Nick. "Kobe Bryant Invented a Word to Describe His New Signature Nike Shoe." *USA Today*, Gannett Satellite Information Network, 7 Feb. 2018, ftw.usatoday.com/2018/02/kobe-bryant-invented-a-word-to-describe-his-new-signature-nike-shoe.
237 Gabay, Jalique. "Nike Kobe 1 Protro Deconstructed: The Makings of Performance Retro." *WearTesters*, 8 Oct. 2019, weartesters.com/nike-kobe-1-protro-deconstructed-the-makings-performance-retro/.
238 "Nike Zoom Kobe 1 Protro Colorways, Release Dates, Pricing: SBD." *Sneaker Bar Detroit*, 16 Oct. 2018, sneakerbardetroit.com/tag/nike-zoom-kobe-1-protro/.
239 Jarrel Harris, e-mail message to the author. August 17, 2020.

240 "KOBE AD NXT 360." *Nike News*, 21 Mar. 2018, news.nike.com/footwear/kobe-ad-nxt-360.

241 "Nike Kobe A.D. NXT 360." *Sole Collector*, solecollector.com/tag/nike-kobe-ad-nxt-360.

242 Moreno, Matthew. "Nike Kobe A.D. Releasing Aug. 24 (Kobe Day) In Multicolor." *Lakers Nation*, 22 Aug. 2018, lakersnation.com/nike-kobe-ad-multicolor-releasing-aug-24-kobe-day/2018/08/22/.

243 Chase, Chris. "Nike Kobe AD Exodus Performance Review." *WearTesters*, 9 Jan. 2020, weartesters.com/nike-kobe-ad-exodus-performance-review/.

244 Chase, Chris. "Kobe Bryant's Nike Kobe AD Exodus Is Now Available for Customization on NIKEiD." *WearTesters*, 25 Sept. 2018, weartesters.com/kobe-bryants-nike-kobe-ad-exodus-now-available-customization-nikeid/.

245 The Corp With A-Rod and Big Cat. "Alex Rodriguez and Big Cat Interview Kobe Bryant - The Corp." YouTube video, 44:39. Posted by The Corp With A-Rod and Big Cat. December 31, 2018. https://www.youtube.com/watch?v=ndGZU2BwAVY

246 "Nike Zoom KOBE IV Protro." Nike News, February 6, 2019. https://news.nike.com/news/nike-zoom-kobe-4-protro.

247 "Nike Kobe 4." Sole Collector. Accessed September 16, 2020. https://solecollector.com/tag/nike-kobe-4.

248 Meredith Cash, e-mail message to the author. August 19, 2020.

249 Twersky, Tzvi. "MAMBA 101: Welcome to Kobe Bryant's Next Chapter ." SLAM, September 12, 2019. https://www.slamonline.com/nba/kobe-bryant-cover-story/.

Chapter 11: #GirlDad

250 Nike. "Kobe Bryant: Don't Change Your Dreams | Birthplace of Dreams | Nike." YouTube video, 1:57. Posted by Nike. August 22, 2019. https://www.youtube.com/watch?v=pZjFpAJfcSY

251 "Built for Speed: The Nike KOBE AD NXT." Nike News, August 8, 2019. https://news.nike.com/news/nike-kobe-ad-nxt-official-images-and-release-date.

252 Ibid.

253 "Nike Kobe A.D. NXT: Nike." Sole Collector. Accessed September 16, 2020. https://solecollector.com/sd/08660/nike/nike-kobe-ad-nxt.

254 @NBA. "@KobeBryant being a dad!" Instagram, November 17, 2019. https://www.instagram.com/p/B4_kMN0g4ac/

255 "This Courtside Moment between Kobe Bryant and Daughter Gianna Showed Their Loving Bond." TODAY.com, January 26, 2020. https://www.today.com/news/kobe-bryant-daughter-gianna-bryant-s-loving-bond-shown-viral-t172524.

256 Chavez, Paul. "Kobe Bryant and Daughter Gianna Sit Courtside to Watch Los Angeles Lakers Game at Staples Center." Daily Mail Online. Associated Newspapers, December 30, 2019. https://www.dailymail.co.uk/tvshowbiz/article-7836471/Kobe-Bryant-daughter-Gianna-sit-courtside-watch-Los-Angeles-Lakers-game-Staples-Center.html.

257 Meredith Cash, e-mail message to the author. August 19, 2020.

258 "The KOBE V Gets the Protro Treatment." Nike News, December 19, 2019. https://news.nike.com/news/nike-kobe-5-protro-chaos-official-images.

259 Santiago, Elliot. "NBA 2K20 Nike Kobe 5 Protro Chaos GE." Sneaker News, December 20, 2019. https://sneakernews.com/2019/12/20/nba-2k20-nike-kobe-5-protro-chaos-gamer-exclusive/.

260 @KobeBryant. "On to #2 @kingjames! Keep growing the game and charting the path for the next." Instagram, January 25, 2020. https://www.instagram.com/p/B7xOgFjnuiO/

261 Kim, Allen. "Nike Released a Touching Tribute to Kobe Bryant on the Day of His Memorial." CNN. Cable News Network, February 24, 2020. https://www.cnn.com/2020/02/24/business/kobe-bryant-nike-tribute-trnd/index.html.

262 @AdidasHoops "The adidas family's hearts are with the families, friends and all those affected by today's tragedy. Kobe was a true legend that inspired others beyond the boundaries of the game. He will be greatly missed. Mamba forever." Instagram, January 27, 2020. https://www.instagram.com/p/B7z7UJzp_y6/

263 McCollough, J. Brady. "Lakers Honor Life of Kobe Bryant with an Emotional Tribute." Los Angeles Times. Los Angeles Times, January 31, 2020. https://www.latimes.com/sports/lakers/story/2020-01-31/lakers-honor-kobe-bryant-life-logo-trail-blazers-fans-staples-center.

264 Chiu, Allyson. "'I'm a Girl Dad': Kobe Bryant's Words Inspire Proud Fathers to Celebrate Daughters in Viral Movement." The Washington Post. WP Company, January 29, 2020. https://www.washingtonpost.com/nation/2020/01/29/kobe-girldad-fathers-daughters/.

265 Quinn, Sam. "The Clippers' Collapse in Game 7 Is Another Reminder That They Still Are Who They Have Always Been." CBSSports.com, September 16, 2020. https://www.cbssports.com/nba/news/the-clippers-collapse-in-game-7-is-another-reminder-that-they-still-are-who-they-have-always-been/.

266 McCarriston Feb 24, Shanna. "Kobe Bryant Memorial: Beyonce, Alicia Keys, Christina Aguilera Perform at Service." CBSSports.com, February 24, 2020. https://www.cbssports.com/nba/news/kobe-bryant-memorial-beyonce-alicia-keys-christina-aguilera-perform-at-service/.

267 Hays, Graham. "Gianna Bryant, Alyssa Altobelli, Payton Chester Selected as Honorary Picks at WNBA Draft." ESPN. ESPN Internet Ventures, April 17, 2020. https://www.espn.com/wnba/story/_/id/29050684/gianna-bryant-alyssa-altobelli-payton-chester-honorary-picks-wnba-draft.

268 Kasabian, Paul. "Nike Announces 1st-Ever 'Mamba Week,' $1M Donation in Honor of Kobe Bryant." Bleacher Report. Bleacher Report, August 13, 2020. https://bleacherreport.com/articles/2904340-nike-announces-1st-ever-mamba-week-1m-donation-in-honor-of-kobe-bryant.

Made in the USA
Monee, IL
11 December 2020